WALKING STILL

From the Heights of the Himalayas
To the Depths of the Mind

MARLA SUTHERLAND

Sushila Press

Cover Design by Brian Swanson Studio
Cover Photo by Marla Sutherland
Author Photo by Terry Sutherland

ISBN-13: 978-0-9981841-0-4

With gratitude

to

Carl and Sylvia Feiles

who gave me life

and

S. N. Goenka

who taught me the art of living

Note to the Reader

This journey took place many years back, and I meant to get the story out there a long time ago. I can only hope that it is better late than never.

Before smart phones and tablets, apps and ATMs, GPS and the internet, it took a different kind of planning and determination to travel the world, especially as a female alone. A map and a guidebook, and maybe a little insanity, were my only companions.

In the ensuing years, the names of many cities in India were changed for nationalistic or political reasons. Thus, Bombay is now Mumbai, Madras became Chennai, and Cochin is called Kochi. However, the names of these and other places are referred to herein as they were known to me when I visited them.

Whether you are an armchair, virtual or actual traveler, I hope you will find some inspiration, maybe a little insight, or just a few hours of entertainment within these pages. It may have been my experience, but it is yours for the taking.

Marla Sutherland
April, 2017

CONTENTS

CONTENTS

Sometimes we think we have found the place, the niche, and my insight is that we should keep on our traveling shoes, that we are in process, every one of us, and we should keep on the traveling shoes and be ready.

Maya Angelou

Once Upon a Time . . .

. . . there was a little princess. All the court loved her, for she could sing and dance quite well. One day she married the prince of a neighboring kingdom, and with great fanfare they began their life together. But there was no "happily ever after," for soon the princess became discontented, and was spirited away by a knight in shining armor on his swift and sturdy steed. They left the kingdom in a cloud of dust and went to live in Lake Tahoe. The princess became a blackjack dealer and learned to ski.

After some time, however, the princess again became discontented, and now she knew that there was no prince or knight who held the key to her happiness. She reached for pills and powders to make her feel better, but they only made her life a mess. Finally, in despair, she plunged into the great wilderness alone, searching for the answer. She did not heed the sign which read "No Turning Back."

For years she wandered thus, until her princess gown was all in tatters. Eventually she found herself on the other side of the world (India, of all places). It was there she met a wise person who helped her understand the reasons for her misery. He pointed out a path to freedom from suffering; a path to self-knowledge and wisdom; a path to inner peace.

And though the journey is long and hard, there you'll find her, walking still . . .

In order to live free and happily,
You must sacrifice boredom.
It is not always an easy sacrifice.

Richard Bach

WALKING STILL

Prologue: Reality Check

My whole life flashes before my eyes. Not just once, or all at once, as it might if I were frozen in the path of an oncoming train, but in a continuous series of instant replays, like an automatic repeat mode, gone berserk. Fast-forward, rewind, fast-forward, rewind. I can't seem to put my finger on the "play" button.

All I want is a little peace of mind. That's what brought me to this meditation center in the first place.

But each time I sit down cross-legged on my cushion and close my eyes to meditate, there it goes again. The movie of my life flashing across the frayed screen of my mind, reel after unrelenting reel, accompanied by a non-stop mental commentary of what I should have done differently before and what I will do differently in the future.

So sharp is the picture, so three-dimensional the view, it is as if each scene is happening this very moment, and there I am, living it again, and again, and again . . .

I came here for sanity, and feel even crazier than when I started.

What on earth was I thinking?

Truth is, I thought this would be a great escape from reality. Step out of bounds, go on an adventure to Asia, slay some dragons, reach nirvana.

Of course (you probably already know this), reality doesn't stop just because you go to a different country, or sit down on a meditation cushion. It just changes.

Turns out that dragons aren't quite how I imagined them. Maybe nirvana isn't either. I don't know about that yet, or if I ever will.

Still, as I struggle to remain calm while the havoc unfolds behind my eyes and pushes at the edges of my psyche, I have a strong sense that this is exactly where I need to be and what I need to do.

So here I sit on my behind, watching the movie of my mind.

Welcome to today's reality.

*In the longing that starts one on the path
is a kind of homesickness, and some way,
on this journey, I have started home.*

Peter Matthiessen

Before the Beginning:
On the Threshold

The international terminal at Los Angeles Airport is like a rolling sea of people and baggage moving in waves toward ticket counters and gates. I look around and wonder where everyone is going on a Tuesday afternoon in the middle of January. It takes my mind off the real question. The one I have been asking myself for days.

Do you have any idea what you are getting yourself into?

Waiting in line at Korean Airlines, I chew off my few remaining fingernails and try to block out the checklist that repeats itself compulsively over and over in my head. I decide to worry instead.

I hope they won't make me check my bags. I've heard that flights to Asia are notorious for "lost" property.

I hand over my passport. Born in the U.S.A. July 11. 7-11. A lucky day. The agent looks from my picture to my face and squints his eyes. The photo was taken three years ago. I was twenty-nine at the time.

Have the last three years left such a deep impression on my face?

Then he pulls out my ticket and asks, "Any baggage?"

I take a deep breath. "Well, if it's all right, I'd like to take both of these on board with me."

He looks at the small blue duffel bag gripped tightly in my hand and the red daypack perched on my back. Then he looks at me again. I smile sweetly. My eyes plead. Nodding okay, he hands back the documents.

"Gate 23 in 30 minutes. Enjoy your flight."

I can barely hear him over my sigh of relief.

Turning away from the counter, I see my father waiting to walk me to the gate. The choking feeling which has plagued me for the last week closes up my throat again. The tears that have swelled at the corners of my eyes for days begin to spill over. I wipe them away quickly, but he still sees the redness. My crying upsets him.

"If it makes you so unhappy, then why are you going?" he asks. "Please, honey, I wish you would consider staying home."

"I'm not unhappy. I'm just a little nervous. Anyway, it's all planned now. I have to go."

"No, you don't. If you want to cancel the trip I'll help you get started again. You don't have to go through with this."

I reach over to caress his balding head and kiss his smooth, plump cheek. He smells like Old Spice.

"Thanks, Dad, but I wouldn't give this up for anything. It's what I really truly want to do. But that doesn't mean I'm not scared."

He looks puzzled. Then he says the same thing he said to me fifteen years earlier, when I left Los Angeles to go to college in San Francisco. "I don't understand why you have to go so far away to learn what you want to know. Why aren't you happy here?"

Good question, Dad. I wish I knew the answer.

At seventeen, determined to go away to school, I had offered the worn analogy of a bird leaving the nest and learning to fly on its own. It was cliche, but true, and he and my mother finally accepted my decision.

Now, at the age of thirty-two, two marriages already behind me, I don't know how to tell him that the ideas I grew up with about the way life was "supposed" to be have left me disillusioned and negative. It would break my father's heart to know how much I have dreamed of happiness, how often I have awakened to discontent.

"Dad," I falter, knowing that what I am about to say may not make any sense to him, "I know it seems crazy to you, traveling to the other side of the world by myself. But this is the first time that I have followed my own inner direction, instead of doing what is reasonable and expected of me."

His eyes are sad. "I just want you to be happy, honey."

I do wish I had a simple answer for him, something concrete enough for him to hold onto; but I have no other answers, even for myself. Only a feeling that moves up from my solar plexus and gets stuck in my throat; a knowing beyond reason that pushes like firm hands at my back.

I board the crowded 747 for the first twelve-hour leg of the journey. The cabin is filled with Asian faces. Large families are stowing luggage and securing children, speaking to the stewardesses in what I assume to be Korean and Chinese.

The plane will land in Seoul, South Korea, where I have a three-hour layover. The next flight is scheduled to stop in Taiwan and Hong Kong before depositing me in Bangkok for a two-day stopover. Then I fly to Bombay, India. At that point, my itinerary becomes vague. I plan to be extremely flexible as I travel "one day at a time" to places of scenic, historical and spiritual interest to me. I hope to learn some meditation and yoga along the way.

When springtime blooms in Nepal, I will make my way to Kathmandu, where I have arranged with an "adventure travel" company to go trekking in the Himalayas.

My ticket is valid for four months. I'd like to stay the whole time.

If I last that long.

As the engines warm up, I wonder if what has brought me this far was actually a vision, or simply a hallucination. I feel fragmented between confidence and fear, and need to find a thread, a connection that will hold the parts together. I buckle myself in, close my eyes, and try to block out the cacophony of strange syllables around me so that I can hear the whisper, see the vision, feel the inner knowing once again.

My thoughts move backward in time six months. I am alone in a red vinyl booth at The Diner in the Napa Valley wine country of California, in my typical Saturday morning pose: a mug of coffee in one hand, a book in the other.

On this particular day, the book is Somerset Maugham's *The Razor's Edge*, and I am deeply immersed in the story. But just as I get to the part where Larry tells Isabel,

> *I can't go back (to Chicago) now. I'm on the threshold.*
> *I see vast lands of the spirit stretching out before me,*
> *beckoning, and I'm eager to travel them . . .*

I am surprised to hear someone call my name. I've only lived in the valley a short time, and I don't know many people.

A fellow with dark curly hair is waving at me from a nearby table. He looks vaguely familiar, but I can't place him. The next thing I know, he gets up and brings his coffee over to my booth.

"Hi! Remember me? Jeff. We met at a wine tasting last week." He sits down. "May I join you?"

Do I have a choice?

"Uh, sure," I say, closing my book reluctantly.

We make small talk about the wineries at which we work. He tells me about his running regimen; I tell him about my yoga class.

I haven't told anyone about the yoga before, or the relaxation meditation we do in class. It's all still pretty new to me. The difference in how good my body feels and how clear my mind has become since I started the class is really uplifting. A pleasant change from the recent downward spiral of a second disintegrating marriage and a frightening dependency on "mental pain killers" in the form of little blue pills and vials of white powder. But I don't want to talk to him about that part.

I give him the good news instead. "I've decided to go back to college after twelve years and finish my degree in Psychology."

No need to share that I really have no idea what I want to do with my life, but that school seems as good a place to start as any.

"Good for you," he smiles. "I'm planning a trip, myself."

"Anywhere exciting?" I ask.

"Australia, New Zealand, Southeast Asia," he pauses, "The World!" and throws his arms up with a laugh. Then he points at me. "Have you done much traveling?"

"Well, nothing as exotic as that. When do you leave?"

"Oh, I don't know," he mumbles. "Whenever I get enough money together."

Then, as if he is sharing a great secret, Jeff pulls a small book from his coat pocket and traces his dream route on a map which unfolds from its pages. I follow his finger until it lands on the small mountainous country of Nepal, nestled snugly between China and India.

A warmth spreads through me, like the glow of still-hot coals. It is connected to a memory, long forgotten.

"I thought of going to Kathmandu, once," I murmur, touching the line of bumps indicating the peaks of the Himalayas.

"Really? Tell me about it."

"It's kind of silly. It started with this movie I saw about a dozen years ago, the old 1937 black-and-white version of *Lost Horizon* with Ronald Colman. I'm not much of a television watcher, particularly late at night, but I had a memory of being entranced by the movie when I was a child, and couldn't resist a strong attraction to stay up until midnight and see it again."

My body starts to tingle, just in remembering, and now I am talking as much to myself as to Jeff.

"It was the story of Shangri-La. A hidden valley in the mountains of Asia. A mythical land of perfect beauty and happiness. I was infused with a sense of magic, and I longed to be there, imagining myself in those mysterious and mystical mountains, the Himalayas."

I pause and laugh at my dramatic portrayal. "That's when the first tiny spark of interest was lit, and it was fanned one day when I picked up a travel brochure in a backpacking store. It described Kathmandu and a trek into the Himalayas of Nepal. Looking at the pictures, I was mesmerized."

My body tingles again with waves of apprehension and excitement as I remember holding the brochure in my hand.

Kathmandu! The name itself had reverberated with magic and mystery, as if calling to me from afar. *Kathmandu.* I knew I had to go there. To the hidden valleys of the Himalayas and the exotic realms of my own mind.

"So why didn't you go?"

"Huh? Oh, well, that was ten years ago. The timing just wasn't right."

I decide not to tell him the truth, that I had thought a trip like that was something only other people did; that such a journey seemed too overwhelming to even consider; that Kathmandu didn't "fit" into my life. The whole idea was too risky. My need for security was too great, my pattern of living up to the expectations of others too ingrained. Kathmandu did not have a place of reference anywhere in my experience, although I couldn't deny that it had a place in a deeper part of me.

"Well, why don't you go now?"

"What? To Kathmandu? You're kidding."

"No." Jeff looks directly at me. "What's stopping you?"

The walls seem to echo the words.

What's stopping you?

I stare at him, speechless for a moment. "People just don't up and hop the next plane to the Himalayas, you know."

13

A wide grin practically covers his face. "Why not?"

I lean back slowly, as his question hangs in the air between us. The walls reverberate.

Why not?

The crackle of the PA system interrupts my reverie as the flight attendant welcomes me aboard and points out the exits from the aircraft. But I am not yet ready for take-off, and allow my thoughts to drift back in time once more.

It is the evening of my conversation with Jeff, and I sit on the small porch outside my apartment, gazing at the first stars shimmering over the lush vineyards. I am convinced that the Napa Valley is a good place for me to have come to heal my personal wounds, to make a fresh start.

The months here have provided time for introspection; an opportunity to reflect upon the past, contemplate the future, and discover what is meaningful to me now. I enjoy the quiet. No music. No television. Silence. I listen instead to the subtle stirrings of myself.

Myriad questions arise from the solitude to fill my thoughts. Questions about the purpose of my life, the notion of who I think I "should" be, the possibility of who I *could* be. And the questions grow in scope of their own accord, wondering about the meaning of *all* life, and the source of creative energy, and who or what is God or Truth?

The answers remain elusive, but just the process of questioning, itself, has begun to fill the hollow void which threatened to consume me from the inside out.

Looking at the stars, I fantasize about traveling to Nepal. I pick up my current yoga magazine, and am drawn into the cover photograph of a holy city in India. I recall again the legend of Shangri-La, feel the magnetism of the Himalayas, hear the mysterious far away call of *Kathmandu*.

I squirm in my seat and wonder how the thought of something so foreign, so unrelated to anything I have ever known, could attract me so strongly?

It's as if that tiny spark has burned through the wall of my conscious mind and is moving slowly through the dark hallway of my subconscious, bringing pinpricks of light to shadowed areas. Not enough illumination to reveal what's there; just enough to let me know that there are corners I have never even thought to explore.

A sudden shiver of fear is calmed by a warming sense of adventure. Exotic images dance inside my eyelids. I open them with a jerk.

"Don't be silly," I chide myself.

A whisper floats through my thoughts.

What's stopping you? It asks, softly.

"It's a ridiculous idea," I reply. "I need to get on with my life. To finish my education. To accomplish something for a change. I can't go traipsing off to the other side of the world on a mystical adventure."

Why not? The voice is a bit clearer this time.

"Well, I finally have some money in the bank, and there's my application for school in the mail. I love this valley, my apartment, and especially my yoga class. I wonder if I could study with a real yoga teacher in India?"

What's stopping you? The volume increases.

"Everybody would think I've lost my mind. It's one thing to pick myself up and move to a new town. But going to Asia?

15

That's quite a different story. I just can't do it."

Why not? The voice is becoming rather insistent.

"I don't know anyone who would go with me. But then, I did go to Hawaii alone last year . . . well that's a far cry from going by myself to the Himalayas. Or is it?"

What's stopping you? It's practically shouting now.

"I don't have the courage!" I shout back.

Why not? The voice is softer again.

"I don't know."

What's stopping you? A whisper.

"Nothing."

At that moment, the long-smoldering spark seems to burst into flame. Its brightness illuminates my deepest longings and clearly reveals my direction. Like a signpost, it points: "Spiritual Pilgrimage."

"What?" I gasp in astonishment. "ME?"

And then I clearly hear the words "WHY NOT?"

This time it is my own voice, speaking the words out loud.

Suddenly my thoughts are racing, fueled by the fire of inspiration.

Maybe it really isn't such a crazy idea. It would be a natural progression of what I've been doing here. An outward journey with an inward focus. I could study yoga and meditation, and I could trek to Shangri-La!

I begin to laugh as an incredible sense of freedom washes through me, clearing away my excuses. Then I talk to the stars.

"The college degree has waited this long; it can certainly wait a while longer. It's time for another kind of education to begin. Time to put myself on the line and trust that inner voice; and while I'm at it, have the adventure of a lifetime."

16

The stars seem to twinkle back at me, and my decision becomes crystal clear.

"I will go to India, and the Himalayas, and . . . yes! to *Kathmandu.*"

As the jet begins to taxi down the runway I hold onto the memory, the vision of my personal pilgrimage. It will help get me through the difficult places ahead, as it has during my preparation for the journey.

I can still see my mother's face as I tell her about my plan. She looks as if she wants to strangle me. "Oy vey! Couldn't you please wait until after I'm dead?"

My estranged husband mocks me when he hears about it. "Isn't that the sort of thing people did in the sixties? Are you looking for a 'goo-roo'?"

My father is behind me, but is disturbed by the fact that his "baby girl" will travel alone. "Who will take care of you if you need help?"

Most everyone else is incredulous. "You're going where? By yourself? No way."

And then there is Jeff, the fellow in The Diner, who with his own dreams inspired mine. He gives me one more gift before he disappears from my life forever. He introduces me to Arlene, a local winery owner, who has traveled to India and Nepal, on her own.

When we meet there is an instant affinity, a comfortable connection, a common thread of Los Angeles Jewish roots. Arlene and I discover that at a turning point in each of our lives we had begun to ask ourselves questions that had no obvious answers. We had also each experienced a strong

17

attraction to Asia and the philosophy of the East; and, upon making the decision to travel there alone, neither of us had found much support for our "spiritual adventure."

Over the next few months, as Arlene shares her traveling stories with me, her eyes sparkle and her enthusiasm is contagious. We meet for lunch, and stay through dinner. When I express doubt about whether I can actually make the journey, she shakes her curly head at my protests. "Of course you can do it. You have to do it."

Along with her unflagging encouragement, she offers one piece of advice and a strong recommendation.

The advice is to "keep a sense of humor (you'll need it)."

The recommendation is that I go take a ten-day meditation course from a teacher in India by the name of "Goenka" (Go-en'-ka). She hands me a faded yellow flyer and urges, "don't forget."

As the day of departure approaches, I carefully pack my small blue duffel bag with clothes and necessities, doing my best to prepare for any eventuality. Into my red daypack goes camera, guidebook, toothbrush, several pens and a blank journal.

I am ready. About as ready as a blind person leaving home without her cane.

The attendants take their seats. The plane lifts off the runway. Cool air shoots out of the vent above my head. So it begins, a journey of the spirit, of the Self. Perhaps I am being irrational, but I'm tired of being rational. All I care about right now is being *me*. And this journey is a creative expression of the deepest part of my being. A new art form: *Living life as myself.*

It often seems that in order to create anew, something else has to be destroyed, or at least allowed to fall away. Is letting go an inherent part of the creative process?

Looks like it's part of mine.

I've left a good job and a nice apartment in a beautiful valley behind. I've also left the residue of broken marriages and addictive behavior, and shelved my plans to go back to college. My belongings are stored away now, awaiting my return. I don't know exactly when that will be. It all depends on what I find, on how I do. The risky part is the uncertainty of not knowing what to expect. But that's the great adventure, too.

Now I know that everything that has come before has been in preparation for this moment. It's as if I am standing on a threshold, opening a door to the rest of my life. On the other side waits the unknown. Will it be a stairway to paradise? Or the edge of an abyss?

All I have with me now of the secure, the predictable and the familiar are a small blue duffel bag tucked neatly beneath my seat and a red daypack balanced on my lap. Even more important are the treasures held close to my body: a passport, some traveler's checks and a ticket to *Kathmandu.*

19

A pilgrimage distinguishes itself from an ordinary journey by the fact that it does not follow a laid-out plan or itinerary, that it does not pursue a fixed aim or a limited purpose, but that it carries its meaning in itself, by relying on an inner urge which operates on two planes: on the physical as well as on the spiritual plane.

Lama Anagarika Govinda

The Buddha and the Trash Heap

Enroute to Bangkok, I stuff a dinner roll and some crackers into my daypack.

My seatmate, John, laughs at me. "Emergency rations?"

I blush. "Well, it might be a long time before I eat again." I'm embarrassed to tell him that I'm afraid I might find the food too strange.

"Here, take mine, too." He hands me his roll with a smile.

John has been a good companion on the last three-hour leg of a nearly twenty-six hour journey. He's from Philadelphia. A carpenter in his mid-thirties. He earns enough money building houses during the summers to spend his winters on the beaches of Thailand, Malaysia or wherever he wants. He says he's hooked on the East, an "Asia junkie."

As we begin our descent, he asks if I have a hotel in mind. I shake my head. "I understand there is a desk at the airport that helps you find a place to stay."

"That's true, but it's risky to take a room sight unseen. Especially at 10:00 p.m. in Bangkok. What kind of a budget are you traveling on?"

"Pretty minimal," I reply, ruefully.

"I usually stay at The Malaysia," he says. "It's a cheap travelers' hotel, but adequate. Do you want me to call from the airport and see if they have a room for you?"

I nod gratefully, glad to have assistance with my first steps on Asian ground.

Customs goes smoothly, and the phone call to the hotel produces rooms for both of us at a rate of eighty *bhat*, four dollars, each. We leave the terminal to find a taxi, and are blasted by an air temperature in the high eighties, with about 90% humidity. John opens the cab door for me with a flourish. "Welcome to Bangkok."

My room is sparsely furnished. A twin bed. A dresser. A family of cockroaches in the bathtub drainer. But the sheets look clean enough and the door locks. I eat a package of soda crackers and take a swig from the bottle of water I purchased at the reception desk. Setting my duffel bag and my daypack next to the bed, I put my valuables under my pillow, as John has advised me to do.

Exhausted from travel, too tired to even think, I am ready to rest. As I lay my head down, I smile. I am cushioned by my passport, some traveler's checks, and a ticket to *Kathmandu*.

In the morning I meet John in the lobby, as planned, excited about my first day in Asia. We walk a few blocks through the tropical heat to a narrow street lined with drab travel agencies and cheap restaurants that cater to "low-budget" and student travelers from the West. Dilapidated buildings, trashy streets, a wild-eyed panhandler. It doesn't look like a great part of town.

"So where's Yul Brynner, 'The King and I', the Royal Palace?" I ask as we sit down at a grimy table and order scrambled eggs, disillusioned that Bangkok doesn't seem too different from any other big city I've visited.

He laughs. "Well, nothing is quite like it looks in the movies. After breakfast we'll go to the outdoor Weekend Market. You may find that more 'exotic'!"

By foot and by bus, through fearsome traffic and noxious exhaust, past glittering Buddhist shrines and dusty roadside fruit vendors, we make our way through the teeming city. An hour later we arrive at the Asian version of a flea market.

Under large canvas coverings stands a disorganized array of goods of every kind. Bamboo cooking utensils share a crowded table with wind-up toys. A variety of umbrellas spill onto a stack of Thai silk paintings. In the "pet" department, parrots squawk from their cages and monkeys scream back from theirs. The narrow aisles overflow with merchandise, leaving little room for the swarms of people to pass through, as vendors aggressively hawk their wares and customers bargain for the best deal.

The smells of popcorn, incense and barbequed delicacies waft through the air. I accept a sample of skewered meat from a small hibachi, but the chili burns my mouth and beads of sweat pop out on my forehead. Much of the other food is unfamiliar to me. One tray looks like it contains sea urchins. I begin to wonder if I will find enough to nourish myself. *I'm glad I have those rolls in my pack after all.*

While walking around with John, I feel confident and wear my Self-Assured-World-Traveler look. When I see a table selling saffron and other enticing spices, I stop for a moment to sniff around. When I look up, John is gone. I search the sea of Asian faces for his Caucasion one, without success.

I feel a tightening in my throat. *Where could he be?*

The jostling crowd seems to close in around me. *There's no reason to panic.*

My heart is pounding. *I'm not ready to be left alone!*

Suddenly I am not at all sure about my ability to survive this journey on my own. I feel like I just want to cling to someone. To know that they will be there for me if I need them.

"Oh there you are!" he says, squeezing by some boys trying on sunglasses. He raises his eyebrows at me. "Are you all right? It's pretty intense, isn't it! But don't worry. You'll get used to it."

With a deep breath, I nod my head. *I hope you're right.* He doesn't know how relieved I am to see him; how much less sure of myself I am than when we started out this morning.

I soon discover that we are not the only western travelers mixed in with the locals at the market. I hear one couple speaking French. Two girlfriends converse in German. They are wearing *batik* fabrics, long wrap-around skirts, thin blouses. They appear to be experienced Asia travelers, like John.

Looking at them, I feel ill prepared and impatient with my naiveté. Now everything that I packed so carefully seems all wrong. Blue jeans and yellow Nikes will stand out like sore thumbs in a world of rubber flip flops and cotton sarongs. My skirt feels too short, my T-shirt too tight. Wrong shoes, wrong clothes, wrong, wrong, wrong.

Or is it just me that's all wrong? I imagine that everyone notices me and judges me as severely as I judge myself.

As we leave the market, I realize that it is time to test my Asia wings – to fly alone for a while. I want to find the heart of Bangkok. To understand why I have come here at all.

I tell John that I have decided to strike out on my own. With my map in hand and the echo of his "good luck" behind me, I head for nearby *Wat Thai*, a group of Buddhist temples whose graceful sloping roofs and vibrant colors are visible from blocks away.

Leaving my shoes outside the entrance, I step inside the Temple of the Emerald Buddha. The wood floor is cool and smooth against my bare feet. The walls are crafted with thousands of colorful mosaic tiles and lined with rows of shimmering golden Buddhas. The Emerald Buddha himself, a delicately carved figure of soft green opaque stone, sits high atop a golden pyramid, enshrined in a small glass case.

The temple is filled with kneeling devotees chanting prayers, eyes closed, each in their own spiritual world. A small Thai woman shuffles by me and magically creates a space in the crowd for herself to sit where there appeared to be none. Her bare feet peek out from beneath her multi-colored sarong as she reverently bows toward the sacred image. Her forehead meets the floor, and stays there for a long time. Finally, she straightens her back proudly, the dark bun of her hair just touching the long nape of her neck, and places her hands softly together in her lap.

My eyes open wide to take it all in, then close tightly for a moment to hold the vision I fear will disappear. There is real beauty here, not only in the surroundings but in the attitude of devotion which permeates the air I breathe.

Standing there, just inside the door, I feel as if a different chord has been struck in the musical score of my being; a set of lost notes which bring to the surface an ache that I carry deep inside, a longing which has remained buried most of my life.

To whom or what could I ever be devoted?
Could I truly surrender?

Memories are stirred of when I was a teenager in Los Angeles. I would make secret visits to the Catholic Church near our house after school and kneel in the empty pews. It was a cavernous place with dark paintings and carvings along the walls, massive stained glass windows and a dramatic crucifix over the altar. I felt small there, and yet so full. But it would have been unthinkable to let my parents know how moved I was by the sense of a presence greater than my own while in the church and not in the synagogue. It would have been even worse to tell them that I had actually thought about converting to Catholicism so that I could become a nun and really know God. I was convinced those women in the long black habits had a direct line, a connection unavailable to a nice Jewish girl like me. And I wondered,

Why aren't there any nice Jewish nuns, anyway?

As I prepare to leave the Emerald Buddha, the lost chord continues to resonate through me. I put my hands together in prayer position and bow slightly, as I have watched the others do. I expect it to be an empty ritual. Surprisingly, it is a strangely humbling gesture, a moment of complete unself-consciousness. It is a feeling that stays with me as I blend into the stream of devotees emerging into the Asian sunlight.

Small groups of monks in orange robes with shaven heads quietly stroll the pathways between the temples. They carry nothing but wooden begging bowls for donations of food, having renounced all worldly possessions in their quest for enlightenment.

The whole place is like a sea of serenity. I would like to

immerse myself in its depths and float to a peaceful state of mind; but I can't imagine how.

Outside the temple walls I am jolted into another reality. The afternoon traffic and noise and smog are thick. These are part of Bangkok's inheritance from the industrialized world. Too bad they didn't inherit mufflers, too.

The open stalls that line the streets sell everything from aluminum cooking pots to paperback books to "knock-offs" of designer labels. Each one has music blaring into the heavy humidity that pervades the afternoon. Fresh cut fruit looks good, but glistens with water, so I don't dare.

I stand aside as a wrinkled and toothless old woman with a wide cone-shaped straw hat negotiates the crowded street. She carries two pails of water suspended by ropes from the ends of a long stick balanced across her stooped shoulders. It is a picture from a country village, or from another time, strangely out of place in the chaos of the city, in the here and now.

On a nearby corner, many people are gathered in the courtyard of a small temple. I watch them each place a thin sheet of gold leaf all over a large golden Buddha sitting on a pedestal. He is becoming misshapen under the heaps of gold which devotees must have been putting on him for years. The wooden table in front of the statue is covered with flowers and burning incense.

A boy offers to sell me a small sheet of the gold leaf for five *bhat*. I suppose if I can bow to an Emerald Buddha, I can add some gold to a golden one. Waiting my turn, I place my square of gold leaf on his arm.

I guess we each have our burdens to bear. Yours is gold. Mine is garbage.

I sigh as I recall describing my "burden" to my friend Ed before leaving for Asia.

"I feel as if I am carrying an incredible weight around with me all the time." I bent over to demonstrate.

"Like the weight of the world on your shoulders?" he teased.

"No, it's more like this huge pile of garbage that I forgot to throw away. And it's starting to smell."

He playfully held his nose. I ignored him as I began to mentally sift through it and describe what I saw.

"What a bunch of emotional trash! First of all there's guilt. Layers of guilt. Guilt and worry over things I've done, things I haven't done, and everything in between. Then comes anger. A lifetime of repressed anger, all crunched up in the fear of rejection. All of that stuff is mixed up with a pile of shoulds and shouldn'ts, feelings of not being 'good enough,' regrets over roads not taken, anxieties about the future, and plenty more, all held together by the gunk of depression. Yuk."

He laughed wryly, but it wasn't funny. I kept going.

"Over time each bit has been stuffed away out of sight and out of mind, so that I don't even remember the particulars. The situation passes, but the junk accumulates and stays with me. It's like a heavy invisible trash heap which has become a congealed mass and sticks to me like glue."

Ed raised his eyebrows and shrugged as if to say 'so what else is new?'

"You call it a trash heap," he said. "I call it my 'bag of shit' – the emotional waste products of my life. I think everybody has one, but I'll bet that most people don't even know it's there, and they don't want to know either. They probably just keep wondering why they are miserable and stuck in the muck of their lives."

"So I'm not alone," I replied. "But that doesn't lighten the load any."

His face finally showed some compassion. "Well, I think it's just part of being human, but you could try hauling the whole thing down to the dump."

I suppose that's where a good therapist comes in. Or maybe a journey, like this one. I have certainly brought my garbage along, as usual. Maybe Asia will help me find somewhere to drop it.

The golden Buddha bears his growing burden with a peaceful smile. People keep piling stuff on him, but he doesn't seem to take it personally. None of it obscures the essence of inner light that emanates from him so radiantly.

I become acutely aware that I grimace and slump under my own heavy load, and that if I radiate anything, it is negativity.

I stand near the shining Buddha for a long time, wondering about the difference in the way we respond to what the world offers us. Something tells me it's more than the fact that he's a statue . . .

What do you know that I don't?

The next evening, John waits in the lobby with me until the taxi pulls up in front of the hotel entrance. He exchanges a few words with the driver before turning to me.

"He'll charge you 100 *bhat* to get to the airport. That's about five dollars," he says, putting my bag into the back seat.

"Thank you. I mean, thanks for helping me out, and everything."

31

Thanks for being there when I needed a life line.

"It's no problem. Have a great time in India and Nepal. They're fantastic places. Pretty soon you'll be an 'old Asia-hand' yourself."

The cab pulls out into a stream of traffic. I clutch my daypack on my lap and turn to look out the back window. With a final wave, John disappears into the hotel and my transitional umbilical cord is snapped.

There is a sudden pressure in my chest and a strangling sensation in my throat.

Oh, God, I can't breathe.

I grip the seat and gasp for air. Just when I am sure I will pass out, I feel as if I am being slapped on the back by an invisible hand. I let out a sharp cry, and with a rasping sound my lungs fill themselves with oxygen. The driver turns to look at me. I smile weakly and shrug my shoulders.

As we weave our way through the night world of Bangkok toward the unknown of India ahead, I prepare myself to survive without a life support system in an alien world.

*If a man wishes to be sure of the road
he treads on, he must close his eyes
and walk in the dark.*

St. John of the Cross

Gateway to India

An attractive Indian girl, about twenty years old, is deeply involved in a movie star magazine when I sit down next to her on the flight from Bangkok to Bombay. Looking up with a smile, she introduces herself as Rina Jahandra and tells me that she is on her way home from Hong Kong.

"I've been visiting my Auntie who lives there and shopping for my trousseau," she says, in a lovely musical accent.

"Oh, you're getting married?" I ask.

"Certainly, someday soon, when the right man is found and the match is arranged. It's important to be ready at the right time, you know."

As we speak, she admires her manicure and examines her make-up in a compact mirror, adding fresh black *kohl* to the outline around her eyes. Her smooth skin is the color of *cafe au lait*. There is a small diamond in the left side of her nose.

Rina holds her head proudly and straightens the collar of her silk blouse. "I have just passed my exams, showing that I am well educated, and my father will provide a good dowry, so it's just a matter of time."

Then she asks where I will be staying in Bombay. I hesitate, uncomfortable about my answer.

"I don't know. I thought I would find a hotel when I get there. I have this guidebook . . ." I hear my voice trailing off as the enormity of my decision to travel alone "one day at a time" begins to dawn on me. Nervous perspiration tickles at my upper lip.

"What? Find a hotel at two o'clock in the morning?" she exclaims. "Nonsense. You must come home with me." Her tone is firm. It is more like an order than an invitation, and I am not sure what to do.

"I wouldn't want to impose on you," I say.

Rina opens her compact for the third time in ten minutes, looks herself over once again and runs a comb through her luxurious long black hair. Then closing the case with a snap, she turns and looks at me intently with her dark liquid eyes.

"You know nothing about Bombay. Letting you go out there alone tonight would be like throwing you to the wolves." Then she reaches over and takes my hand. Her voice softens. "Really. I insist that you come home with me."

How can I refuse such an offer when I truly don't have any idea of what I am getting myself into?

I smile and nod my thanks. She pats my hand in reply, picks up her magazine again and a moment later is engrossed in the secret affairs of a famous Indian actor.

At the Bombay airport, Rina's parents recover quickly from the bombshell that I will be staying with them.

Her bespectacled father is dressed in western style slacks and shirt, while Mrs. Jahandra wears a traditional blue silk sari.

36

Rina's eighteen-year-old brother, Ravi, is in a pair of white Indian cotton "pajamas." They all speak at once in a mish-mash of Hindi and English.

It is 3:00 a.m. before Customs finishes examining my two small bags and Rina's five large suitcases filled with clothing and lingerie.

Finally, the five of us and all the baggage are somehow packed into the family car. As we roll away, her father proudly explains that it is a "late model" Ambassador automobile, manufactured domestically. To me, it looks more like a 1954 Plymouth, or a large green turtle on wheels.

I crane my neck around the piles of luggage hoping for a glimpse of Bombay. The darkness of the sleeping city is pierced only occasionally by a small fire glowing on the street, surrounded by groups of people talking or sleeping. My first introduction to the homeless of India.

We drive to the southern part of the city near the waterfront. Mr. Jahandra points out one of Bombay's principal landmarks, the Taj Mahal Intercontinental Hotel. The lights from the lavish lobby softly illuminate the figures of a mother and child huddled on a street corner. I am surprised by an ache in my heart, a rush of sympathy and sadness.

I thought I was mentally prepared for this. Maybe it's not possible to be emotionally prepared. . .

Upon our arrival at the family's large third floor apartment, I am surprised to see an old woman, curled up fast asleep in her cotton sari on the living room floor.

At the command of Rina's mother, she jumps up and begins to race around, turning on lights and carrying bags into bedrooms. I am told that Kamala is the household servant as well as the family's cook.

I am ushered through a blue gauze curtain into a large room with several low, contiguous beds. Two of them are occupied by Rina's other brothers, who are unceremoniously awakened and moved out to other rooms. Ravi stretches himself out on the living room floor in the same white cotton pajamas. I feel guilty about taking over the boys' bedroom, but they seem to think nothing of the intrusion.

Once in my nightshirt, I sit down on the orange-red sheet and look around in vain for some kind of cover. I ask Rina, who is preparing to sleep in the next bed.

"What do you mean, silly? It's much too hot to cover up. Oh, here, have a sheet if you must."

Wrapping myself up, I lie awake for a long while, my inner time clock askew, my body exhausted, my mind racing.

I made it. I'm here in India. I'm really here.

Dangling my arm over the edge of the bed, I stroke the small duffel bag sitting on the floor and pat the daypack perched on top. My valuables are safe here, and so am I. A light breeze blows in through an open window, ruffling the curtain door. Watching it flutter, I finally drift off to sleep.

In the morning I watch as Kamala squats on the cement kitchen floor to chop ingredients, grind spices and roll out dough, as she must have been doing for years. But the old kerosene burner beside her appears to have been replaced by a "modern" stove (circa 1950 or so) and an electric rice cooker.

After a breakfast of buttery scrambled eggs, white toast and sweet milky tea, Rina takes me out for a tour of the city and some shopping. Our last stop is a large Hindu temple, which is unlike any other place of worship I have ever been. It is like a gallery of psychedelic art, and no one is still.

The worshippers move around the temple offering incense, sweets, money and prayers to several animated, florescent statues adorned with garlands of orange flowers. All of the images display unusual and even startling features such as extra arms, eyes or heads ("*Brahma* has four heads because he sees all," Rina tells me), various skin colors ("The bright blue one with the flute is *Krishna*, all the girls love him"), and the head of an elephant on the body of a boy ("You pray to *Ganesh* for good fortune").

The three major Hindu deities, *Brahma*, the "Creator," *Vishnu*, the "Preserver" and *Shiva*, both the "Destroyer" and the "Reproducer," carry the most weight in the spiritual hierarchy, but the Hindu pantheon is populated by scores of other gods and goddesses. The intricate cosmology that relates each of them to the other supports one of the most ancient religions in the world.

I watch as parents teach even their littlest offspring to perform various rites and rituals in the temple, having them kneel in front of the brightly painted statues, chant prayers, make their offerings of candy and coins and sprinkle themselves with holy water three times.

No wonder they start so young. It probably takes a lifetime to understand it all.

Again I find myself admiring acts of devotion. But I am not drawn to participate in these rituals. For me, the atmosphere in the Buddhist temples in Bangkok was like a serene lake in the morning calm. The mood here among the colorful

Hindu deities and their numerous devotees is more like crashing ocean waves at the onset of a storm. After a short while of being fascinated with the activity, I am ready to leave.

Outside the temple gates the deformed and diseased are begging. I imagine they gather at the temples knowing the devoted are more likely to contribute. Mostly men, they are afflicted with elephantiasis or shriveled limbs or no limbs at all. I wonder if it is true that some have been mutilated purposely to create a more pitiful picture and therefore earn more money.

There, but for the grace of God, go I.

But how different are we, really, the beggar and I? Beyond the physical, the external circumstances of our lives, the perceived limitations of our existence – isn't there more about us that is the same than different?

"From ashes thou come, to ashes returned."

All we are is dust in the wind.

Down the street, a thin, dark skinned woman in a faded green cotton sari draws a picture on the sidewalk with colored chalk and bits of sparkling glitter. As she squats there, spindly legs sticking out at angles, long arms reaching with sweeping motions, the lovely image of a goddess comes to life on the ground before her. People passing by throw donations of small coins on the picture. This creation of temporary art must be her devotional practice and her livelihood. I drop a coin. She doesn't notice. As if in another world, she allows her inner vision to take form on the pavement below.

For dinner, Kamala prepares wonderful dishes of chicken and lamb curry, steaming rice and vegetables. She also makes a flat bread called *chapati* and a puffed bread called *puri*. Her home-

40

made yogurt cools my mouth when the food is too spicy for me. I am given silverware to use, but try to eat like the rest of the family – scooping it up with my fingers.

During the next two days, each time Rina and I return to the apartment from an outing, I find that my laundry has been done. The generous hospitality of the whole family is a great gift to me; yet, at the same time, I feel like a novelty for them to have around and display to their friends and relatives, who come in groups to meet me.

Look! We have an American lady who's over 30, not married, no children and traveling the world all by herself staying with us.

I begin to understand that the word "privacy" is unknown in this overpopulated country. People are always together – close together.

On my second afternoon in Bombay, I tell Rina that I am going out for a walk.

"Alone?" She looks astonished. "Whatever for? If you must get out, I'll come along with you."

Thanks a lot.

She doesn't comprehend that I am alone by choice. But I don't mean to be ungrateful. It is my good fortune to have met her. My transition into India has certainly been a smooth one, almost as if the way were gently paved for me.

Later, I do finally leave the apartment alone, and wander around the nearby grandiose Taj Mahal Intercontinental Hotel. While visiting the fancy "Western style" ladies room, I take a roll of toilet paper to add to the small supply I brought from home. T.P. is quite a luxury here, and not found in many public places because most Indians don't use it.

Asian squatting toilets are set into the floor, with little

41

indents on either side for the feet. There is a small water faucet low on the wall nearby. The water is to clean oneself after using the toilet (this is done only with the left hand — the right hand is used for eating). Washing is actually a more effective method than wiping with regards to cleanliness, but much less appealing to my conditioned Western mind.

I will continue my search for toilet paper.

Stopping for fresh coconut juice at an open-air street stall during my solo meandering, I realize that I am already feeling at home with the exotic flavors and pungent smells of India. However, there are other aspects of being here which are not so comfortable for me.

Sometimes, out on the street, I experience a disturbing vibration which makes me want to shake off my skin, and the air around me feels charged with a powerful force. There is so much unseen, unknown energy flowing in every direction, and in the worst moments it feels like I am walking through an atmosphere of writhing snakes.

Also, there are the beggars. Even more plentiful, more pitiful, than I expected.

Across the street from the Taj Mahal Hotel at the edge of the waterfront is an imposing arch called the Gateway of India. As I look at the plaque inscribed, "A Symbol of British Pride — 1911," I am approached by several bony children with outstretched hands. Their sunken eyes are pleading, their voices thin.

"Baksheesh?"

A ragged child of six or seven years old holds a baby on her hip. The infant is naked except for two red plastic bracelets on her wrist. I had heard that parents send their children into the streets to beg because adults cannot resist them. I find myself wondering if beggars have "territories."

The hotel must be a good area to work.

As I reach into my pocket for change, a dozen more waifs appear as if by magic. Suddenly I am surrounded by a pack of children clamoring *"Baksheesh! Baksheesh!"* They close in all around me, dirty fingers pulling at my clothes. In desperation I throw the coins down on the ground, push my way out of the circle and walk hastily away down the street. I glance back to see them splitting up the take.

Around the next corner, a leper with stubs for fingers and two holes where his nose should be reaches out to touch me in his plea for money. Fearing contact with his sores, I pull back angrily and glare at him. But in return, I see only a compassionate smile on his cracked lips and pity in his eyes for me.

What? Why does he feel sorry for ME?

I am convinced that he is in the worst possible situation, but he continues to look at me with incredible kindness, as if I am the one who is poor and incurably sick. His response throws me into confusion.

Could he be right?

Do my reactions of fear and anger eat away at my spirit as surely as leprosy consumes his flesh? Is the heap of emotional garbage I carry just as destructive to my being as the burdens of poverty and disease are to his body?

He puts his palms together near his heart and bows slightly, as if thanking me, although I have given him nothing.

"Namaste'," he says. It sounds like a blessing.

I begin to wonder which of us is actually the poorer.

He slowly glides away, but I am unable to move. My perspective is jarred, like a small earthquake of the soul; and through the crack I am given a view into the heart of India, granted a visit with her true character.

Eventually roaming the choked streets once again, I find myself aware of much more than the harsh physical realities of poverty and disease. I watch the strong help the weak, and the weak help the weaker, and I see that there is more than meets the eye in these difficult, dynamic surroundings. The subtle layers of compassion and devotion which lie hidden just beneath the heartbreaking surface must give nourishment to the soul even as the body goes hungry. How unfortunate that visitors who denigrate India for her filth and poverty do not shed their judgments long enough to look beyond her external appearance and be rewarded by her inner beauty.

Overwhelmed by the vast differences between this culture and my own life in the United States, I am also overwhelmed by the magnitude of my decision to make this journey, alone.

I return to the Taj Mahal Hotel and her sparkling lobby populated by Arab men in traditional headdress, Japanese businessmen in dark suits and fashionably dressed European tourists. The extremes are confusing to my overwrought senses. I decide to make my visit to the big city a short one.

The next day I purchase a bus ticket to Aurangabad. It is the nearest town to the ancient temple caves of Ellora and Ajanta, the next "planned" stop of an unplanned journey.

When I announce my departure and thank them for their hospitality, Rina and her family admonish me to be careful "out there" and encourage me to return to Bombay. I assure them that I will do so.

The bus departs at 9:00 p.m. The green vinyl seats are narrow and cracked, the motor noisy, the road in disrepair. I put my towel behind my head and use a sweatshirt for a blanket, doing my best to get comfortable for the next ten hours.

The all-night ride leaves me sore and tired, but what greets my eyes alongside the road as we pull into town is captivating.

So this is the face of India.

I see golden brown skin, a long white beard, and bushy white eyebrows almost completely covering dark, piercing eyes. The hair on his nameless face stands out like contrasting patches of snow upon a red clay hill. The tail of a white turban hangs loosely over the shoulder of his once-white shirt, and a length of white material called a *dhoti* is tucked up around his spindly legs. He sits on his haunches, smoking and looking. A face such as I have never seen; a life story written in its creases. India begins to come alive for me.

Aurangabad is a dusty town, more like a large village. Emaciated holy cows are given the right of way on the roads and pigs grovel around in open sewers. It is one of the many mysteries of Hinduism to me that cows are more sacred than people, who may be dying of starvation even as meat walks the streets. Yet who am I to question the meaning of something I know nothing about? Religion and life are intertwined in India, and if one has enough devotion, death is nothing to fear.

The townspeople talk and laugh together around smoky cooking fires on the streets and gather in the little shops which line the dirt roadways. Wrapped in soiled clothing, they gaze at us as we pass by in the bus. Waving forlornly, a little girl looks as if she longs to climb aboard, bound for anywhere.

45

Ox-drawn carts pull heavy loads, children pull at their mother's breasts, people live in corrugated tin shacks or tents made of grass and sticks.

Is this life? Or just existence?

Ellora and Ajanta. I think those would be beautiful names for children.

The setting of the Ajanta caves is sweepingly dramatic. They are cut into the steep curved face of a rocky gorge similar to some American Indian cave dwellings in the Southwest U.S.A. But these caves were not used as residences. They are Buddhist temples and monasteries dating from as early as 200 B.C. I pay an attendant five rupees (about fifty cents) to shine a light on the fading ancient frescoes, and am jostled by throngs of Indian tourists and school children on field trips. It is too popular, and too noisy a place for me. The crowds in the caves make me feel claustrophobic, and I hurry outside for fresh air.

Several miles away, I am relieved to find the caves of Ellora more peaceful. I also experience them as more intimate. There are several protected niches for me to sit and think; to feel where I am.

The tall sculptured temples, carved out of solid rock from the top down, were created over the ages by Hindus, Buddhists and Jains. Each group has a unique artistic style. The Hindu caves feel charged with the same dynamic energy of the streets and temples of Bombay. The Jain caves amaze me with their incredible workmanship; every wall is decorated with minutely detailed friezes. But it is the Buddhist caves which draw me in the deepest with their atmosphere of calm contemplation. Resting in front of a large seated stone Buddha, I feel at peace,

46

and quite at home.

My subsequent encounter with the Aurangabad Railway Station provides a sharp contrast. Humanity coats the floor. People eat and talk, build small fires and play with their children. It is hard to tell if they are waiting for trains or live in the station. Several bodies are wrapped in blankets which cover even their heads in order to rest undisturbed. Dreamers, or corpses? Again, hard to tell.

I wait in a long, slow-moving line to buy a train ticket to Igatpuri. The town is the location of Mr. Goenka's meditation center, where I have decided to follow the advice of my friend and take a ten-day course in Vipassana meditation. Hopefully it will be peaceful there.

A uniformed station agent approaches me.

"Ladies may go directly to the head of the queue, Madam." I look around and see that there are only males in the line. They look back at me curiously. It is obvious to me that women usually do not purchase their own tickets, much less travel alone. Self-consciously, I squeeze past all the men and go right up to the window.

I had planned to do all my train traveling by second class to conserve money; but novice that I am, I decide upon a first-class ticket for my first train ride in India. Just the accomplishment of the purchase itself in the chaos of the station feels like a victory.

The clerk hands me the ticket and looks kindly at me with his serious dark eyes. "Have a good journey, Madam."

I thank him and realize, after only four *days* in India, that my time frame of four *months* is probably not enough to even scratch the surface of this geographical, cultural and spiritual giant. Four *years* might be more realistic . . .

One thing is fairly certain: we usually select the known, seldom the strange. We tend not to choose the unknown which might be a shock or a disappointment or simply a little difficult to cope with. And yet it is the unknown with all its disappointments and surprises that is the most enriching.

Anne Morrow Lindbergh

"May All Beings Be Happy"

The train leaves Igatpuri station with a series of whistle blasts. Standing on the platform, surrounded by magazine vendors and the tea sellers known as *chai wallas*, I wonder which way to go. I cross the pot-holed street to a kiosk which displays cigarettes, flashlight batteries and ballpoint pens. Not sure if the proprietor speaks English, I simply say the name of the meditation center.

"Dhammagiri?"

With a serious look on his dusty brown face he replies, "No, Madam. This is not *Dhammagiri."* Then he breaks into a smile, glad to have put a joke over on me. He points out the way, first with a straight finger, and then indicating several turns. After that it's easy. I just keep following the direction of friendly fingers, obviously used to pointing the way to the many visitors who come to learn meditation from Mr. Goenka.

Winding my way through the narrow bustling streets of Igatpuri, I pass the outdoor barber giving a shave with a straight-edged razor and peek into the ramshackle shop of a tailor sewing diligently on a foot-powered treadle machine. The street market merchants weigh fruits and vegetables on balance

51

scales, and the shoe vendor urges me to buy a pair of cheap rubber flip flops. (I walk away with blue ones.). The smell of frying food and the beat of taped Indian music accompany me as I make my way up a low hill at the edge of town and finally reach the gates of *Dhammagiri*, the Vipassana International Academy.

I am welcomed to the meditation center by an Australian woman, registered into the upcoming ten-day meditation course and given a place in a crowded women's dormitory with the luxury of mosquito netting around my cot. I sit on the bed and pull the net closed. It gives me the illusion of privacy from my neighbors.

Once my duffel bag is stowed beneath my bed and my daypack hung on a hook nearby, I sit outside on the steps to the dorm and shield my eyes from the afternoon sun. I am surprised at the large number of people at the center, and the variety of nationalities. Apparently people come from all over India, as well as North America, Australia and Europe. I catch bits of a variety of languages as they stroll the quite pathways.

Many of the "Westerners" seem to know each other, maybe from having been here before. They chat together happily and look comfortable and at home in their cool, breezy Indian cottons.

Out of my comfort zone again, and unsure of what to expect, my sense of being "a stranger in a strange land" is even stronger in this spiritual center than in the teeming streets of Bombay. My shoulders hunch defensively, my jaw is tight.

Eventually a long-haired blonde girl wearing a soft white blouse and a flowered sarong wrapped around her waist notices me sitting alone and comes over.

"Hello," she says, in a lovely British accent. "My name is Anne. Your first time here?"

"Yes," I admit, and introduce myself. I also admire her clothing, complaining that my blue jeans are too heavy for the sultry weather.

"They won't be very comfortable for sitting meditation, either," she observes, her face crinkled in thought.

The next moment, she grabs my hand, saying, "There's plenty of time before the course begins. Let's go to town and get you a few things."

Bless you, Anne.

I'm given a lesson in friendly bargaining as I watch her strike the deals for my few purchases. Anne is patient with me and patient with the shopkeepers. She seems so at ease in India, in her clothing, even in her body. By comparison, I feel awkward and adolescent. I wonder how I can be more like her.

Maybe my new clothes will help.

I return with an Indian cotton shirt and some wraparound fabric called a *lungi,* which keeps falling down because I haven't learned how to tie it correctly. But back at the meditation center I am still uncomfortable, and I know it has nothing to do with my clothes.

It's an old familiar feeling. A feeling of being superimposed over a photograph of life, and not actually part of the scene. An isolated person separate and disconnected from everything else in the world. Floating in an invisible cocoon, untouchable, unable to touch.

I long for a sense of harmony. To be an integral part of the whole picture. To feel at home.

Can being here possibly take me there?

I stretch out on the narrow bed and am comforted by the presence of my duffel bag under the springs and the daypack hanging on a nail in the wall.

My passport and ticket have been put away somewhere in a safe. I miss them.

I decide to read the booklet I was given upon my arrival.

Introduction to
VIPASSANA MEDITATION

May your meditation here prove most beneficial to you. We offer the following information with all good wishes for success.

Vipassana (vip-a'sana) is one of India's most ancient meditation techniques. Long lost to humanity, it was rediscovered by Guatama the Buddha more than 2,500 years ago. Vipassana means "insight": to see things as they really are. It is the process of self-purification by self-observation.

Does that mean I don't see things as they really are now? Must I be "pure" to have insight? In that case, I'm in trouble already.

The entire Path (*Dhamma*) is a universal remedy for universal problems and has nothing to do with any organized religion or sectarianism. For this reason, it can be practiced freely by all without conflict with race or religion in any place, at any time and will prove equally beneficial to one and all.

I'm glad of that. Religion is certainly not what I seek - but what do I seek? (Aside from a good supply of toilet paper, of course.)

What Vipassana is not:
It is not a rite or ritual based on blind faith.
It is neither an intellectual nor philosophical entertainment.
It is not a rest cure, a holiday or an opportunity for socialising.
It is not an escape from the trials and tribulations of everyday life nor an asylum for disgruntled misfits.

Disgruntled misfits? Sometimes Indian English makes me chuckle. But otherwise this is beginning to sound like a serious place.

What Vipassana is:
It is an art of living which frees the individual from all the negativities of mind such as anger, greed, and ignorance.
It is a practice which develops positive, creative energy for the betterment of the individual and the society.

Those are pretty big claims. Could it really be all that? Sounds like a panacea. Why does that make me skeptical?

The rules should be carefully read and considered.
Only those who feel that they can honestly follow the discipline scrupulously should apply.

Uh oh. Here goes.

THE CODE OF DISCIPLINE

The Five Precepts:

All who attend a Vipassana course should observe rigorously the following five precepts:

1. To abstain from killing any sentient being.
2. To abstain from stealing, i.e. from taking that which is not given.
3. To abstain from all sexual activities.
4. To abstain from telling lies.
5. To abstain from all intoxicants.

I can't remember if sentient means simply being alive, or having the perception of being alive, i.e. consciousness. Is a mosquito aware of its existence? If I slap at them in self-defense am I breaking the law?

Noble Silence:

Meditators must observe Noble Silence from the start of the course until 10:00 a.m. on Day 10. Noble Silence is silence of body, speech and mind. Any form of communication, whether by physical gestures, written notes, sign language, etc. is prohibited. However, the student may speak with the Teacher or the managers whenever necessary. Students should cultivate the feeling that they are working in isolation.

Does talking to myself count?

The booklet goes on to discuss other rules and regulations regarding physical exercise, modest clothing, cleanliness, and the prohibition of reading and writing materials.

It also stresses the importance of complying with the Teacher's instruction and guidance, and indicates that courses are run solely on a donation basis.

I finally reach the last page. . . *what's this?*

THE TIMETABLE

4:00 a.m.	Morning wake-up bell
4:30-6:30 a.m.	Meditation either at your own place or in the meditation hall
6:30-8:00 a.m.	Breakfast break
8:00-9:00 a.m.	**GROUP MEDITATION IN HALL**
9:00-11:00 a.m.	Meditate at your own place or in the meditation hall
11:00-1:00 p.m.	Lunch and rest
1:00-2:30 p.m.	Meditate at your own place or in the meditation hall
2:30-3:30 p.m.	**GROUP MEDITATION IN HALL**
3:30-5:00 p.m.	Meditate at your own place or in the meditation hall
5:00-6:00 p.m.	Tea break (tea and fruit)
6:00-7:00 p.m.	**GROUP MEDITATION IN HALL**
7:00-8:00 p.m.	Teacher's discourse in hall
8:00-9:00 p.m.	**GROUP MEDITATION IN HALL**
10:00 p.m.	Lights out.

MAY ALL BEINGS BE HAPPY

Hmmmmmmm. We're looking at about 11 hours of meditating per day here. Eleven hours per day? For ten days?!

While it's true that I can sit and do nothing longer than anyone I know, these requirements feel pretty extreme.

Do I leave right now, or just stick it out and see what happens?

I decide that the time has come to give in to the fact that I have been inexplicably drawn to contemplation and meditation for a long time, and here we are, looking each other in the face. Again, like the journey itself, it feels as if I have come to this place not by choice, but by direction.

But that doesn't make it any easier.

Ten days. Silent. Sitting on a cushion on the floor. Hour after hour. It will be like removing myself from the face of the earth for ten days. Where will I emerge? Who will emerge?

I find myself standing on another threshold to the unknown.

Will I float into nirvana on the other side? Or sink deeper into the quagmire of my mind?

Meditation is not a means to an end.
It is both the means and the end.

J. Krishnamurti

A Noble and Elusive Goal

All of the students who have come to attend the meditation course are gathered outside the large circular pagoda on the Plateau of Peace. A light shines at the top of the central spire, softly illuminating the curved building in the darkening evening. It is like a beacon shining through the heavy mist of my thoughts.

At 8:00 p.m. a ripple of anticipation spreads through the hushed group as the doors to the meditation hall open outward. Some names are read quietly, and several students enter to take their seats on cushions in the front rows. A few minutes later the rest of us are told to file in silently. The men are directed to enter by one door and sit on the left, while the women go through a separate door and occupy the right side of the hall. I leave my shoes in the growing pile outside and claim my seat on one of the numerous cushions on the floor. Soon the large hall is filled to capacity.

As we all settle down in the crowded rows, I look around. There are about 250 people of various shape, size, age and country of origin. The women outnumber the men, and it looks like the Western population outnumbers the Indians, too.

After several minutes I realize that a man in white clothing sits cross-legged on a dais in the front of the room. His round, clean-shaven face is dark, his silvery hair closely cropped, his eyes set deeply beneath bushy brows.

Must be the teacher. Go-en'-ka.

Hands folded in his lap, he slowly surveys the congregation, and then gently closes his eyes. I close mine too, and let the mood of silent contemplation envelop me.

Without warning, he begins to speak. His voice is deep and rhythmic, the tempo dramatically slow.

"You have all come here to learn *Vipassana* meditation. *Vipassana* means 'insight,' to see things as they really are."

He repeats some of what I had read earlier in the introductory booklet, stressing that the *Dhamma* he teaches is a universal path that can be practiced by one and all, without conflict with any religion or belief system.

Then he asks us to repeat after him:

"I take refuge in *Buddha*" – not a person, he says, but the quality of enlightenment.

"I take refuge in *Dhamma*"– not any religion, but the law of nature, the truth.

"I take refuge in *Sangha*" – the community of people who walk the path of liberation from all suffering.

"I surrender myself to the technique and my present teacher."

At that one I balk, and listen as everyone else drones the words. I am not prepared to surrender. I'm not even sure what it means to surrender, but I imagine it as giving my power over, and that scares me.

62

Next Goenka has us repeat after him the five precepts to abstain from killing, stealing, lying, sexual activities and intoxicants during our stay. By this time it's about 9:30 p.m. and I'm feeling sleepy. My rear end is tired from sitting on the flat pillow which cushions it less and less from the hard floor as the night wears on, and my knees and back are beginning to ache. But we aren't finished yet.

The teacher gives instruction in *Anapana* meditation, which he says is a preliminary practice to develop concentration of mind. We are told to close our eyes and become aware of our breathing.

"Observe your breath at the entrance of the nostrils, as it comes in, as it goes out."

Just that. Nothing more, nothing less.

We meditate for a while. I am able to concentrate on my breath for brief periods, when I'm not nodding off.

Finally at 10:00 p.m. he tells us to "take rest."

With a sigh of relief, I stretch out my legs and roll my shoulders. My sandals are buried in the sea of shoes outside. A quick search uncovers them, and I stumble sleepily to the dorm by flashlight. Rows of silent women are preparing for bed. Falling gratefully onto my cot, I pull the mosquito netting closed and sink into slumber.

It seems only moments before the sound of a gong reverberates through my sleep.

What? What time is it?

Reaching for my watch, I see the awful truth. 4:00 a.m.

Sleeping bodies begin to stir. I procrastinate, and doze again. The gongs are louder this time. I sit up and check the time. 4:30 a.m. Time to be in the hall, meditating.

The morning is icy cold. I pull on my jeans and a sweatshirt, splash water on my face at the communal sink outside, and head for the *Dhamma* Hall by flashlight.

Shivering on my cushion, I try to remember Goenka's instructions. "Observe your breath. Be aware of your breath as it comes in and goes out." I hug my legs to my chest for warmth. "Watch your breath." I rest my forehead on my knees for just a moment . . .

Huh? What happened? I must have fallen asleep. I need to go back to bed. It's freezing in here.

As I leave the hall I notice with envy the warm woolen shawls wrapped around some of the students. Others simply use blankets. Of course. Why hadn't I thought of that?

I'll be sure to bring mine with me, right after I sleep under it some more.

More gongs, big ones this time. Time check. 6:30 a.m. Breakfast.

Silent lines of women and men. Separate eating areas. Mealy lukewarm cereal. A crunchy unfamiliar fruit. The spicy milk tea called *chai*. Then a visit to the bathroom. Squatting toilets with faucets. I begin to ration my toilet paper.

By the time the 8:00 a.m. gong rolls around, I feel much better. Freshly brushed teeth, a crisp morning walk and a cozy blanket/shawl make all the difference. Now I'm ready. But for what?

Everyone settles onto their cushions again. I arrange and rearrange my legs in various positions, trying to get comfortable on the floor.

Just then the side door to the hall opens. Goenka enters, sits down cross-legged on the raised platform and closes his eyes. I look at his neatly parted gray hair, his full cheeks, his round body. The clean white cotton clothing he wears is unadorned. No beads. No flowers. He doesn't fit my picture of a "guru" with flowing locks, like the photo of the Beatles' Maharishi on the cover of Time magazine in the 1960's. In fact, in different attire, it would be easy to mistake him for the successful businessman I heard he was before changing his vocation to meditation teacher.

Suddenly the dark eyes open and look at me as if to say, "Why are you watching me when it is your breath you are supposed to be observing?"

I look down quickly in embarrassment at the non-verbal reprimand.

Okay, kiddo. Let's get serious here. Close your eyes. Watch your breath. As it comes in. As it goes out. Gee, it's warm in here. Guess I can take this blanket off now. Maybe I can put it under me for padding. This cushion is beginning to feel like a rock. I'm getting hungry. Wonder what's for lunch. Hope it's better than breakfast.

Goenka's clear voice cuts into my rambling thoughts. "Just observe. Observe the natural flow of your breath at the entrance to your nostrils, coming in, going out. If the mind wanders away, bring it back gently to observing the breath."

Guiltily, I wonder how he knew that my attention had wandered away from my breathing. I resolve to be more diligent.

One breath. Two breaths. That's better.

I knew I could do it. I just wish sitting like this wasn't so uncomfortable. And no reading or writing or talking for ten days! Isn't it time for lunch yet? I can't wait to get to Kathmandu. Hey! You're not watching your breath!

Again and again I try to pay attention to my breathing. "As it comes in. As it goes out." Again and again I become distracted. I can barely focus my mind on that seemingly simple task for even a moment before it takes a hike into the woods, watches an old movie or sings the same song over and over again. It wanders away into the past, into the future, into fantasies and dreams. Anywhere, but to my breath.

Finally, Goenka does some chanting, and what feels like an interminable period is over. I stretch my cramped legs out in front of me and rub my stiffening neck. My stomach growls softly. Certainly it is time for lunch. I look at my watch. A realization dawns slowly in my stupefied brain.

The time is 9:00 a.m.

After a ten-minute break, we begin again. There will be two more hours of meditation before the lunch break. Goenka repeats the same thing over and over in a calm and patient voice. "Just observe. Be aware of the breath, the natural, normal breath, as it comes in, as it goes out."

I make a heroic effort to concentrate. My mind does not cooperate. Each time I notice that it has drifted into thought or reverie, past or future, I bring it back to attention. "Observe the breath. As it comes in. As it goes out." But soon my mind won't pay attention for even the length of a single breath.

As the morning wears on, my concentration diminishes and my impatience grows. I am irritated with myself, my undisciplined mind, the cushion on which I sit, the teacher and his "just observe," and everything else about the place.

If I have to sit here one more minute, I will go crazy.

Before I realize what I am doing, I stand up and leave the meditation hall.

The only refuge around here is my bed, I decide, as I stomp down the pathway to the dormitory. And that is where I stay, dozing off and on until the gong announces that lunch time has finally arrived.

The silent lines of men and women file into their respective seating areas. I am served a thick lentil soup called *dal*, plain white rice, overcooked okra and the flat bread *chapati*. My worst fears are confirmed.

I will starve to death before I reach enlightenment. Or Kathmandu.

The afternoon is hot, the meditation hall stifling. Perspiration drips from beneath my breasts. I struggle to concentrate my meandering mind on observing my breath, with minimal success.

I begin to wonder who's in charge here anyway? I am breathing. I want to watch my breathing. My mind does whatever it can to distract me from watching my breathing. It replays scenes from my life in great detail. It imagines possible situations arising tomorrow, next week, next year. It writes endless letters and poems. It does all of this without my blessing, even over my objections. My mind has a mind of its own.

The heat rises in the hall, and I am cooking in the oven. As my body and mind reach the boiling point, I go out and douse myself with water.

No way will I go back in there, nirvana or no nirvana.

I remember that when it isn't the hour for "group meditation in the hall" I am allowed to meditate in my own place. I return to the dorm and see the woman next to me meditating on her bed behind the mosquito netting.

So I'm not the only one.

I sit on my cot and close my eyes. *Watch your breath. Please just watch your breath. As it comes in, as it goes out. There's one breath. Two. Good. Very good.*

A few breaths later I think I deserve a rest, and decide to lie down for a minute. Soon the sound of gongs vibrates through my dreams. *What lovely music.* Some time later, I hear them again. Opening my eyes, I glance at my watch. Three hours have passed. *Uh oh. I slept through the afternoon meditation in the hall.* It's 5:00 p.m. Time for tea and fruit.

It is hot and I don't feel like drinking *chai.* I pick up a banana and a small orange. Then I notice glasses of lemonade on a side table, and reach for one. The server says quietly, "The lemon water is for the old students only. They do not take food after noon."

Hmmm. That's interesting. The more time you spend here, the less you get to eat.

That reminds me about Anne. I feel like I could really use a friend, even if I can't talk to her. I look around the dining room and along the pathway, but don't see her anywhere. Dejected, I return to my dorm and sit on my bed.

A light breeze cools the air as the gong announces the end of break and the beginning of the next meditation hour in the hall. I lower myself to the cushion once again, close my eyes, hear Goenka's voice. "Observe the natural, normal breath, as it comes in, as it goes out." Why is that so difficult?

Sometimes I can grab the attention of my mind for a few moments by breathing harder than normal. The rest of the time it does whatever it darn well pleases, from reciting nursery rhymes to listing all the boyfriends I ever had, in order.

It chastises me for sleeping away the afternoon, compares me to a donkey, and asks me what the hell I think I am doing on that cushion.

Seeking enlightenment?

Ha! My own mind calls me a silly fool.

I'm beginning to believe it's right. Confused by the division going on inside myself, I wonder what indeed I am doing here.

What is the point of this, anyway?

A barely audible inner voice replies, *Wait and see.*

Oh, you again. You're the one who got me into this in the first place. Where have you been, anyway? No answer. *Hmfph.*

The day is salvaged by Goenka's discourse in the evening. I realize I'm not the only one in the crowded hall having trouble, for his words can't be directed to me alone. But he describes me to a "t."

"The first day is full of great difficulties and discomforts. The mind is like a wild monkey that will not be tamed. "

That's putting it mildly.

Everybody laughs, clearly relating to the example, and the laughter offers a welcome relief. But underneath the comedy, there is seriousness.

"The goal of this technique is to purify the mind, to free it from misery by gradually eradicating the negativities within."

Could this really be a way to get rid of the emotional garbage that seems to weigh me down so heavily?

"The breath is a tool with which to explore the truth about oneself," he explains. "It acts as a bridge between the conscious and unconscious minds; a bridge which can take us from the known to the unknown."

He encourages us to overcome obstacles, like drowsiness, aches and pains, and self-criticism. "If you continue to work properly, all these difficulties will gradually diminish. Tomorrow will be a little easier, the next day more so."

I rub my aching knee. *I hope he's right.*

I admire his obvious intelligence, his articulate style, his broad white smile and deep, full laugh. He seems kind, sincere and incredibly patient. But enlightened? I am doubtful. My mind interjects. *Do you expect him to illuminate the room, or what?*

The day has been long, full of frustration and discomfort. But I think there is something important for me here. I know my determination has to become stronger than my desire to get up off my cushion and go back to sleep, or I will never learn about what Goenka calls the *Art of Living.* "How to live peacefully and harmoniously within oneself and to generate peace and harmony for all others."

A noble, and elusive, goal.

Destiny is not matter of chance,
It is a matter of choice.
It is not a thing to be waited for,
It is a thing to be achieved.

William Jennings Bryan

This Will Also Change

At 6:00 a.m. the second morning, Goenka quietly enters the meditation hall where I am fighting the urge to crawl back to bed, and losing the battle. He sits upon the dais, puts his hands in his lap, and closes his eyes.

Slowly I become aware of vibrations moving in waves all around me. I open my eyes and look at the teacher. He is wrapped in a wool shawl and sitting perfectly still. But something about him is not still. And then I know what it is.

The vibrations are coming from him!

They caress me in a light massage, moving around and through me, touching deep places inside. Lonely places. Sad places. Places where I have never been touched. Places I have longed to be touched.

Then Goenka begins to chant. His bass voice is unbelievably resonant, rich and unrestrained. It seems to rise from the very depths of his being and flow in spirals throughout the room.

The ceiling, the walls, the corners of the hall are imbued with the extraordinary sound. And so am I. My body relaxes, my mind becomes still and I can almost feel my heart expand.

Wow. Just wow.

I am filled with the most powerful, most healing sounds I have ever heard.

Throughout the rest of the day, Goenka instructs us to observe our breath at subtler and subtler levels, becoming aware of the lightest touch where it passes into the nostrils, and out again.

He urges us to "keep on working, keep on working diligently."

While I work, my mind plays. I become annoyed, agitated. My body stiffens from sitting cross-legged on the floor. My head starts to pound each time I close my eyes and try to watch my breath. The coughs, sneezes, burps and farts of my neighboring meditators are like fingernails of irritation scratching a blackboard inside me.

As the day wears on, I sleep more and meditate less. Worse than that, I wake up from my naps feeling guilty and angry. And when I sit down to meditate after tea break, I hear about it. My mind is relentless.

What did you come here for, to sleep for ten days? This is nothing but a waste of time. You never finish anything you start, anyway. Like college, or learning to play the guitar, or even marriage.

Ouch. That was a low blow. Just watch the breath. Please.

It's true and you know it. You don't have the guts to stick this out. You would rather run away than risk failure. That's why you're here isn't it? Pilgrimage, shmilgrimage. You are afraid to face real life as a responsible human being.

Wait a minute! Who are you? What are all these voices in my mind?

74

Sharp little pains shoot through my knees. Pins and needles stick in my feet. Lead weights push my shoulders toward the floor. I want to cry out, but a steel band tightens around my chest, compressing my lungs.

Help me!

And then, as if in answer to my plea, Goenka begins to chant.

A huge fiery ball of sun sinks low in the sky. The sound of the gong reverberates through the still warm air. Students drift slowly out of doorways and float down the path to the meditation hall. I feel part of a living stream, flowing silently, following a direction set by nature itself.

"The second day is over. You have only eight days left to work," begins the evening's discourse.

It is good to have a chance to lighten up and smile during Goenka's talk. It is particularly funny when he attempts to use American slang to color his stories. The whole hall rocks with laughter.

I also find something humorous in the man himself. Maybe it's the way his body jiggles like Jell-o when he laughs or the lilting sing-song quality of his Indian English. It all helps to remind me that even though he is up there on the dais, he is an ordinary human being, like myself.

Somehow that makes me feel better because I have so much resistance to the idea of a religious leader. I don't like the fact that most of the students bow down to him at the end of meditation hours. If there is one thing I know, it is that I am not willing to bow to anyone.

Goenka talks about what the Buddha taught:

Abstain from unwholesome actions.

Perform only wholesome actions.

Purify the mind.

That's all?

"That's all," he answers my silent question. "Nothing more, nothing less."

But what does it mean to purify my mind?

"You spend plenty of time washing your body," he says. "Now it is time to cleanse your mind. *Vipassana* will be the soap you use to remove the impurities of the mind."

I like his analogy. Maybe this really is the place I can clean out my burden of mental and emotional trash. If I can only stay awake long enough.

He explains about the Buddha's Eightfold Noble Path, divided in three parts:

Sila : Morality. The five precepts we have taken.

Samadhi : Mastery over the mind. Learning how to concentrate. What we are doing now.

Panna : Wisdom. We'll learn more about this tomorrow.

He concludes the talk by stressing, "continuity of practice is the secret of success."

My heart sinks. Sleeping is the only thing I have done continuously since I have been here. I am still unable to meditate for more than 30 seconds at a stretch.

Here I am searching for inner peace, and thus far I've discovered nothing but agitation. Two days are over. Eight more to go.

Eight more days? To watch my breath and keep my mind in the present moment? At this moment, all I want to do is go home.

76

Things start looking up on the third day. My body still feels tortured and tied up in knots, but the voices in my mind begin to quiet down.

Along with the awareness of breath, we are now to focus on any physical sensations we feel around the nostrils and upper lip. Tingling, itching, whatever – and not react. Just observe the sensation for as long as it lasts.

I am proud when I do well, like meditate for two minutes or so, straight. But I have to wonder how the "old students" up in front can sit so still for hours while I continually rearrange the position of my legs, fluff my pillow, stretch my neck from side to side, straighten my back and roll my shoulders. It's hard not to compare myself and I inevitably feel inadequate. To top it off, I am constipated. Not quite what I expected from India.

As a matter of fact, the whole thing is a far cry from what I expected of meditation. But I should know better than to expect anything.

Many months ago, during our marital separation, my former husband expressed to me his disappointment in some indiscriminate behavior I had been engaging in at the time. Suffice to say, it had to do with sex, drugs, and rock and roll.

"I really expected 'more' from you," he chastised with a frown.

I surprised myself with a reply from some untapped inner wellspring of wisdom (or maybe a Chinese fortune cookie): "To open the door with expectation is to invite disappointment inside." Even he was momentarily impressed.

Still, I really didn't expect the course to be such hard work. *My family and friends think that meditating is blissfully relaxing. If*

77

they only knew. I'm working harder than ever, and enjoying it less.

I feel a wry smile contort my lips.

Looks like the joke's on me.

I wonder if the result of this work will be worth the effort. I have asked myself that question before, especially with respect to staying married. But I didn't work very hard toward finding the answer to that one, and I still feel guilty.

It is true. I never do things that are hard for me, and rarely follow through with anything I start. Instead I just turn to something else for distraction. Or simply run away. The easy way out has been my method for getting through life.

"The third day is over. You have only seven days left to work. Til now you have been following the five moral precepts and learning to concentrate the mind with the awareness of breath. Tomorrow you will be given instruction in *Vipassana* meditation. Tomorrow you will enter the field of *Panna* – wisdom."

Goenka explains that there are three types of wisdom:

1) The wisdom acquired by hearing or reading the words of another.

2) The wisdom gained by one's own rational, intellectual analysis of the information heard or read (not simply accepting it in blind faith.)

3) The wisdom which develops within oneself at the experiential level. Self-realization of the truth.

Then he tells a story which clarifies for me exactly what he is talking about:

A man hears or reads that the food at a particular restaurant is very delicious, and accepts that it is true.

This is wisdom acquired through another's words.

He goes to the restaurant and sees many people enjoying their food. Based on this, he believes the food must in fact be very delicious. This is wisdom gained by one's own intellectual analysis.

He orders dinner and tastes the food himself. The food is indeed very delicious. This is wisdom at the *experiential* level.

"It is only when he has tasted the food for himself that he has developed his own wisdom. Not because somebody else said it was good. Not because after examining the facts he believed it was good. But because he discovered it was good *through his own experience.* "

The teacher goes on to stress the importance of "experiencing for ourselves" the true nature of all things in order to develop our own wisdom — for that is the road which leads from misery to happiness. And, he says, the true nature of all things is *anicca* (ah-nee'cha), a word from the ancient language of *Pali,* which is what the Buddha spoke. *Anicca* means "impermanence."

Goenka says that no matter how solid anything on the material or mental plane seems to be, the truth is that everything is ephemeral, made up of sub-atomic particles that arise and pass away every moment; constantly changing, moment to moment.

Science has proven that everything in the world is made up of moving particles, and that the rapidity and continuity of the process create the illusion of solidity, or permanence. But according to the teacher, mere intellectual understanding of this reality is not enough.

"It is only when we experience personally (taste for ourselves) the truth of our *own* impermanence – *anicca* – that true wisdom begins to arise."

I straighten up from the semi-reclining position into which I have sunk and listen more carefully.

"When I look at something, it appears to stay the same. This is the apparent reality. But the ultimate reality, the truth, is that nothing stays the same for even an instant in the physical world. There is no solidity in the material world; it is nothing but combustion and vibrations, arising and passing away like tiny bubbles in a champagne glass. This process of change goes on without my control and regardless of my wishes."

Okay. So the changes are so subtle or so fast that we are not aware of them as they are happening. What does that have to do with meditation and agitation and sitting on this cushion hour after frustrating hour?

Goenka reiterates, "Only when one experiences personally the reality of one's *own* impermanence does one start to come out of misery."

How's that? Wouldn't increased awareness of my mortality make me even more miserable?

"As the understanding of *anicca* – impermanence – develops within oneself, another aspect of wisdom arises: *anatta* – no 'I,' no 'mine.' How can I possess or control anything in the material world, even my own body? It keeps changing, growing, decaying, regardless of my wishes.

"Then the third aspect of wisdom develops: *dukkha* – suffering. If one tries to possess and hold on to something which is changing beyond one's control, then one is bound to create misery for oneself. Attachment to what is ephemeral is certain to result in suffering."

Finally, Goenka puts it all in a nutshell.

"The greater the attachment I have to anything, the greater my misery will be when I am parted from the object of my desire. For, according to the law of *anicca*, impermanence, we will eventually be parted. Either it will change, disintegrate or die – or I will."

A chill runs through my body, which has always been a sign for me of hearing the truth.

It's like grasping at a mirage and coming up with an empty hand. There really isn't anything I can hold onto, no matter how badly I want to.

I begin to put two and two together.

If I weren't so attached to things (possessions, people, ideas, even myself) in the first place, then I wouldn't experience the anger or sadness or pain when we were parted. I know that there is a direct correlation between how much I want something and how upset I am when I don't get it. But how can I not have desires? Isn't that just a human characteristic?

"Unwanted things will happen in life. Wanted things won't happen. Good, bad or otherwise, the ups and downs of life are only temporary conditions in the process of change. Come out of illusion, delusion. Come out of craving and aversion. To live a happy and peaceful life you must learn to accept the reality as it is every moment, with equanimity – a balanced mind, a calm mind – without wishing it to be different. This is the path of liberation."

I shift on my cushion as understanding shifts into place.

Goenka is saying that the key to real happiness, as opposed to the fleeting joy that comes from having a desire temporarily fulfilled, is to accept the reality exactly as it is from moment to moment, whether it is pleasant or unpleasant, painful or pleasurable, understanding that it will all change

81

anyway. And that this meditation is the way to learn to do that.

His voice begins to slow at the end of the long talk. The lights in the large hall dim slightly, creating a deeper quiet in the already silent room. Goenka closes his eyes and raises his right hand as if in blessing. With a voice more compassionate and loving than I would have thought humanly possible, he intones, "May all beings be liberated from their suffering. May all beings be peaceful. May all beings be happy . . . be happy. . . be happy."

The old students chant in reply, "*Sadhu, sadhu, sadhu.*" ("Well said, well said, well said.") They bow and touch their heads to the floor.

I walk slowly in the light of the full moon back to my small bed, trying to absorb it all. It is almost too much to comprehend. I feel with every iota of my being that this is the truest, most important thing I have ever heard. I believe all of it, based on his guidance and my own observations, even if I haven't come close to "experiencing for myself." But I am willing to run on the fuel of intellectual wisdom for a while, until the wisdom of self-realization hopefully kicks in.

I know that I will have to make great effort, because it is already clear to me how my own life has been affected by not having the insight of which Goenka speaks.

My thoughts accompany me to bed and keep me awake.

By my continuous dissatisfaction with things as they are and my desire for them to be different; by my attachment to my image of myself, and to my judgments, ideas and beliefs; and by my craving for certain people and things which I thought I couldn't live without (most of which are no longer even part of my life), I have created so much misery for myself and others.

I sigh deeply.

How depressing. Is there any hope for me here? I really think there is, but I just don't know yet how to surmount all the piles of mental debris and emotional shit which block the way.

A mosquito buzzes at my ear, caught with me inside the netting.

It will take a lot of determination to walk this path. Not the false bravery of running off on an 'adventure' to India, but the courage of a warrior.

It is not the path which is the difficulty;
Rather, it is the difficulty which is the path.

Soren Kierkegaard

The Load is Lightened

During the morning of the fourth day, there are a few moments when I succeed at not reacting to the antics of my unruly mind. I simply bring my awareness back to my breath and the subtle sensations below my nostrils. There is less irritation. More calmness. A sense of relief. It is as if the absence of any reaction gives me deep, true rest.

At 3:00 p.m. the tension in the meditation hall is palpable. It is time to receive instruction in *Vipassana* meditation. Even in the envelope of silence into which I have been folded, something tells me this is the turning point of these ten days.

Goenka begins to chant. The vibrations fill the room, charging the air, tickling my skin. In a deep and serious tone, he tells us to focus with more awareness than ever on the point of concentration, the sensations at the entrance to the nostrils.

Then he instructs us to switch our concentration away from the nostrils and up to the top of the head.

I am lost. I can't feel anything at the top of my head. I go back to my nostrils and focus, trying again and again to feel the top of my head. It is blank.

"You might feel an itching or a tingling sensation; maybe tension, or even numbness," says the teacher. "It might feel like ants crawling, or pins pricking."

What am I doing wrong? All I feel is a tremendous pressure bearing down on the top of my head and a number ten headache coming on.

"Could be pressure, or even pain. Any sensation will do."

At that, the pressure lifts and the headache recedes. I realize that those are the sensations of the moment, and wish something more pleasurable would show up.

Then he instructs us to move our awareness slowly down from the top of the head throughout the entire body. As we pass our attention through each individual part of the body we are to notice all the different ordinary bodily sensations that come up everywhere and not react to them.

"Whether pleasant or unpleasant, painful or pleasurable, observe each and every sensation without reaction. Just observe their changing, impersonal nature with equanimity – no craving, no aversion, a balanced mind.

"In this way," he continues, "gradually the entire law of nature, the *Dhamma*, the Truth, will become clear to you."

"*Anicca.* Changing. *Anicca.* Impermanence." Goenka intones over and over again, in his full, deep voice.

Right. My poor body feels like it's tied up in knots and my knees are on fire. I can recite 'anicca, anicca, this too shall pass' all day long, but it's not passing fast enough to please me.

It is difficult to stay still. I wiggle around on my cushion, re-folding my legs and piling padding under my knees, as quietly as possible. At least I am aware of sensations in all parts of my body, painful though most of them may be.

The 90-minute session ends when he leaves the room.

There is a collective sigh of relief as everyone gets up slowly, stiffly, and makes their way out of the meditation hall down the hill for tea. This has been quite a day so far. I can't imagine what comes next, but it doesn't take long to find out.

At the beginning of the six-o'clock group meditation, Goenka drops a bombshell.

"From now on, during the three one-hour group meditation periods here in the hall each day, you will be asked to find a position that is comfortable for you and maintain it, without opening your legs, your hands, or your eyes, for the entire hour."

What? Sit still the whole time? That's impossible.

"These are called *Addithan*, or sittings of great determination."

I just don't think my determination is that great.

"Work diligently," he says. "You must work out your own salvation. Work continuously. Continuity is the secret of success."

Swallowing a moan, I start again, at the top of my head.

After about ten minutes of this first "sitting of great determination," my foot is asleep and my ankle feels broken. I must move. Slowly, quietly I open my legs and change my position. I last about another ten minutes before having to move again. It is an hour that feels like three.

But while I am not able to sit perfectly still the whole time, I am able to keep my reactive mind in check and do not become upset with myself. Each time a position becomes too uncomfortable, instead of bouncing around on my cushion in my usual fashion, I observe the unpleasant sensations for as long as I possibly can. Then, without frustration, or guilt, I make the choice to move. I have a strong sense that losing the unconscious reactions is the key to finding my freedom.

Goenka reaffirms that for me in his evening talk. As everyone settles down for the discourse, he slowly scans the hall, back and forth, like a lighthouse beacon.

"The fourth day is over. You have only six more days left to work."

First, he reiterates the law of impermanence, *anicca*, that throughout the universe, within the body as well as outside it, everything keeps changing.

Then he takes it a step further by telling us that *nothing* is a final product. "Everything is in the process of becoming. Being, changing, becoming, being . . and everything, every change, affects something else.

"Each change has a cause, which produces an effect; and that effect, in turn, becomes the cause for another change – an endless chain of cause and effect."

Okay, I think he's talking about *Karma*.

In the sixties, people spoke of good karma and bad karma as an explanation for whatever happened in life. I thought it was more like "luck." Now I am hearing that, based on the law of cause and effect, there are no isolated incidents. Nothing happens accidentally.

"As the cause is, so the effect will be. As the seed is, so the fruit will be. And as the action is, so the result will be."

Then he tells one of his stories to illustrate the point:

Two seeds are planted in the same soil: one of sugar cane, the other of neem (a very bitter tree). They receive the same sun, the same rain, the same fertilizer.

The sugar cane grows with the quality of sweetness.

The neem grows with the quality of bitterness.

This is the law of nature. No matter how much you pray for the bitter tree to give you sweet mangos, it will not work. If you want sweet mangos, you must plant the seed of sweet mangoes.

As the seed is, so the fruit will be. Our ignorance is that we do not pay enough attention as we plant our seeds.

Suddenly a light clicks on in my head, bright yellow and animated like a cartoon image, with little lines of illumination sticking out all around.

Uh Oh. The implications of this are very big. The seeds of my past actions (cause) have resulted in my current situation (effect), during which my present actions (cause) will determine my future (effect). In other words, I create my own future crop of happiness or misery, based on the seeds planted by my present actions (or reactions). I am 100% responsible.

I let that one sink into my consciousness. But it doesn't have to go very far before I understand what is at the depths.

It means that I can no longer blame anyone else for my unhappiness.

It is clear to me that I have planted plenty of thistle seeds during my lifetime, and still expected a rose garden to bloom. I have lied, stolen, and worse. I have broken every one of those five moral precepts during my life. As a result of my actions, the weeds are rampant, and I often have sharp stickers in my feet. Worse than that, I have left a lot of stickers around for other people to step on.

What a poor gardener I have been! Can I possibly begin to plant seeds of joy instead of negativity? Will I ever harvest the fruits of happiness to enjoy with others instead of the misery I have propagated for so long?

91

Goenka goes on to explain that there are three types of actions: physical, vocal and mental; and that one who learns to observe oneself soon realizes that the mental action is the most important, because this is the seed – the action that will give results. Although it seems that physical and vocal actions should have a stronger effect, they are only the outward projection of the mental actions. So, "mind matters most!"

To understand this more fully, one must know how the mind works; and he describes the four main parts of the mind:

Vinyana: consciousness, or cognition.

Sanna: perception, or recognition

Vedana: sensation

Sankhara: reaction

It works like this: Each time the mind comes in contact with any sense object (a smell, a sound, a sight, a taste, a touch, a thought) consciousness arises. Oh, a smell! Oh, a sound!

Next, the mind perceives what the object is and gives an evaluation (the smell of apple pie: good, the smell of garbage: bad; words of praise: good, words of abuse: bad).

Every evaluation results in a sensation on the body (good evaluation: pleasant sensation; bad evaluation: unpleasant sensation). And every sensation results in a reaction (pleasant sensation: I like it! I want more! thereby creating craving and attachment; unpleasant sensation: I don't like it! No more! thereby creating aversion, hatred.)

The mind is constantly reacting to these sensations, and we are unwittingly caught up in a cycle of wanting, not wanting, craving, aversion. It is through these unconscious mental reactive patterns, or *sankharas*, that we sow the seeds of misery (bitter neem or sharp thistles) instead of planting those of happiness (sweet mango or fragrant roses).

In this way, Vipassana also teaches one how to die peacefully and harmoniously, because one can only learn the Art of Dying by learning the Art of Living: how to not be a slave to our reactions, but become master of the present moment, thereby creating our own future filled with happiness, even until the very last moment of life.

Oh dear. How can I change the ways of a mind that clings to things it likes and runs away from things it doesn't like, thoughtlessly scattering seeds of misery in every direction?

Goenka always seems to know when I am asking myself a question. He answers, using himself as the example.

"While practicing *Vipassana*, if I can maintain the awareness that every sensation I experience is *anicca*, impermanent, and so maintain a balanced, equanimous mind by not *reacting* to any sensation, I can change the habit pattern of my mind. By eliminating *reaction*, which is almost always negative, I have the opportunity to take *action*, which is always positive, and see the resulting positive effects in my life."

Aha. All at once I can see the point of practicing the meditation technique!

First, it is to learn to concentrate and quiet the mind to the point of being able to observe the constant change – *anicca* – going on within myself, and therefore gain insight into the true nature of the impermanence of all things.

Second, and more difficult, is to learn to accept that reality, exactly as it is, with equanimity, a balanced mind, without wishing it to be different.

Two parts: awareness and equanimity. That is the pathway to peace. *But is it possible?*

93

His dark recessed eyes close at the end of the discourse, the right hand is raised. "May all beings be peaceful. May all beings be liberated. May all beings be happy . . be happy . . be happy."

The old students chant in reply, "Sadhu, Sadhu, Sadhu." They bow their heads to the floor.

After the discourse I am able to sit still for a little longer at a stretch and observe sensations throughout my body with a calm and balanced mind. A short-lived success.

The next morning I can't keep my attention anywhere, become frustrated with my mind and aggravated with the pain in my knees and leave the hall to go back to sleep in my bed.

The word "failure" keeps coming up, accompanied by strong feelings of doubt. I know that what I have heard and understood is valuable, but intellectual understanding isn't enough to keep me on my cushion when the going gets rough.

I doze fitfully, my sleep invaded by dreams of a thorny, tangled garden growing out of an immense pile of garbage.

Later on, during the afternoon hour-long group sitting, each minute seems like an hour. My body nags at me. My mind taunts me. A neighbor's sneeze sends a sharp bullet of vibrations through my body.

Every other minute or so I am convinced the hour must be over. The teacher must have forgotten about the time.

I'm going to open my eyes for just a second and take a little peek at my watch. No, no! Don't do it. But I'm sure it's more than an hour. Doesn't he know how painful this is? Don't worry. He knows. Take some deep breaths. It's got to be over soon.

It isn't over soon.

What am I doing here? This is crazy. How can he say we must eliminate craving, and then tell us to 'keep trying, work harder.' That's like craving the elimination of craving! If I don't move I'll go insane.

The throbbing throughout my body becomes unbearable. My knees and back are burning. Even breathing hurts. Just when I think I will faint, Goenka's voice breaks through the screaming silence chanting "*Anicca*" and signaling that the hour is finally over. I bite my lip to keep from crying out with relief.

As I open my bleary eyes, straighten my paralyzed legs and stretch out my compressed neck, I realize that although my mind had gone completely nuts, my body had remained perfectly still. I give myself a mental pat on my aching back.

One small hurdle. One great accomplishment.

"The fifth day is over. You have only five more left to work."

Goenka explains that most suffering is the result of attachment to one of two things. The first is the attachment to craving itself: "I get bored, want a change, want more, never satisfied." Here comes another story:

A man lives in a cozy cottage and is very happy. But how long happy?

His friends have much larger, nicer houses. So he also buys a beautiful house. Now he is happy. But how long happy?

Soon he must have beautiful furniture for the beautiful house. He buys all the furniture. Now he is happy. But how long happy?

His neighbor has a big television and a stereo. He must have these also. Then only will he be happy. But how long happy?

95

He used to take the bus to work. But a man with such a beautiful house and furniture and television and stereo should not have to take the bus to work. He must have a car. He buys a small car. He is happy. But how long happy?

Soon it is as if the car is full of scorpions, biting him. He needs a bigger, better car. A BMW. A Mercedes. He gets a better car. But how long happy?

He needs a Rolls Royce. A fleet of Rolls Royces. A helicopter. An airplane. A space ship!

There is no end to the madness of craving.

The second kind of attachment is to the concept of "I" or "Mine" - the Ego. He gives a simple example:

"If I drop my watch and it breaks, I cry. If you drop your watch and it breaks, I don't cry. I tell you that you should have been more careful! No one cries for the breakage of a watch. They cry for the breakage of 'my' watch. MY watch!"

He expounds further on this by saying that our image of ourselves, our ego, affects everything we do and feel.

"We even love others because of how they make US feel," he explains. "They support our ego. When that ego gratification no longer exists, we stop loving them and look for someone new. But we must learn to love with pure compassionate love, rather than ego-centered love."

That's a lofty ideal. How on earth is a person ever supposed to choose a mate?

On the sixth day, after lunch, I reorganize the contents of my duffel bag, fiddle with the stuff in my daypack and straighten up my bed. Then I do it all over again. I am agitated, filled with negative thoughts and crying for no apparent reason.

I have signed up to have a noontime appointment with Goenka, and join several other students quietly waiting outside the teacher's residence, a little house near the meditation hall. Finally it is my turn, and I am motioned up to the porch, where he sits in a chair, smiling.

I kneel down on a cushion in front of him, take a deep breath, and release it with an involuntary sob.

"What's going on here?" I cry. "I came to find out about peace!"

"It's like the pus coming from a wound," he says gently. "This is what happens when you begin to observe your mind. It's part of the purification process. Sometimes it takes a long time to get rid of all the negativities. Take some rest. Then go and meditate some more."

He smiles beatifically. "Be happy."

Happy?

I turn away, even more agitated than when I had arrived.

Happy! Ha! I have a giant boil so deep inside me that it can't even come to a head to begin to drain. Just aches like hell. The thought of it bursting and the crap pouring out is frightening.

Into my mind comes an image of that invisible "bag of emotional shit" I have brought along on this journey, getting ready to explode and bury me in my own mental excrement.

"The sixth day is over. You have only four days left to work."

Tonight Goenka talks about doubt.

"By this point you may be having doubt about the teacher, doubt about the technique, doubt about your own ability.

Doubt is a great hindrance. Do not let it keep you from your work."

I recognize myself in his words. Not only am I sure that I do not have the ability to do the meditation properly with any consistency, I have begun to wonder why I am abusing myself with physical torture and mental agitation. And I still don't like the religious overtones, especially students bowing down to him with praying hands. But my skepticism is not strong enough to break my commitment to make it through the entire ten days.

I may be a failure at reaching nirvana, but I will not run away this time.

The one thing I do not doubt is the sincerity of the teacher. *Goenka-ji.* That seems to be a term of respect and endearment used by students who go up and ask him questions after each evening's discourse. I have not had the nerve to do that, but I like sitting there and listening to his answers. After the "doubting" discourse, there are many questions.

One student goes up and asks the teacher what he thinks about "past lives" and reincarnation.

Goenka smiles. "Whether or not you have lived before is not your concern. Learn to live this life well and you will not have to be worried about what comes next!"

The questions and answers go on and on. I am so impressed by his depth of good will and tireless efforts, it is as if I have just noticed him for the first time in six days.

I am reluctant to leave his presence. When I finally walk out of the hall at 9:30, exhausted, he is still there answering questions, patiently, "smilingly," lovingly.

By the seventh day, my battle with sleepiness is over. I no longer hide out in my bed avoiding my meditation cushion. My mind and I seem to have reached an agreement. It will wander for a while, writing poetry or letters home, and I do not get upset. Because I am not angry, it won't stay away too long, coming back to focus attention on the changing sensations throughout my body.

Hmmm. Just like a child. Reverse psychology.

The pains in my knees and ankles come and go, sometimes sharp and jagged, other times dull and throbbing, always different, changing, impermanent. Whenever I react to the discomfort with irritation, anger or a readiness to run out of the hall, I hear Goenka's strong, gentle voice. "Make it a choiceless observation. Like observing someone else's pain, not yours. This will also change. *Anicca. Anicca. Anicca.*"

In the evening he talks about refusing gifts:

"When someone brings you a gift you don't want, such as anger, guilt, animosity, etc., do not accept it. Say 'No Thank You.' Take and give only gifts of loving kindness."

Is there a way to return all the gifts of criticism, of Jewish guilt, I grew up with?

The more I listen, the more I comprehend the reverence the old students have for their Teacher. Goenka has become important to me, too, and I recognize that he is an extraordinary human being. His qualities of tolerance, patience, compassion, selfless giving and the commitment to helping others find peace are rare, indeed.

The fact that I have even become so aware of him, at last, is a good sign for me. My mind was so full of rubbish that I probably couldn't have recognized the qualities of enlightenment in a person if they hit me in the face. But there are subtle changes happening in me: a lightening of the emotional load, a stripping off of an outside layer, a pulling back of an inner curtain – a tiny awareness of impermanence and a modicum of equanimity.

Signaling the end of the discourse, Goenka closes his eyes and raises his right hand slightly, palm facing outward toward us, toward me. "May all beings be happy. May all beings be peaceful. May all beings be liberated, liberated, liberated."

I hear my voice join the others. "*Sadhu, Sadhu, Sadhu.*" Well said, well said, well said.

Without thought, without judgment, my palms touch together near my heart as I lower my head to the ground.

The foolish reject what they see,
not what they think.
The wise reject what they think,
not what they see.

Huang Po

A Healing Balm

My spontaneous act of bowing to the Teacher brings along with it a sense of lightness, of freedom, of joy in the letting go of the need to be right. With the bow, the walls of doubt, resistance and fear also come down.

When I had thought I needed the "courage of a warrior" to do this meditation, I thought it meant that I would have to fight. But the courage required of me, as it turns out, is the courage to stop fighting.

Surrender. A difficult concept for a mind so skeptical, so secretly angry, so attached to being independent. What a surprise it is to discover that surrender in a spiritual sense is not about giving myself up, but about giving up my ideas about myself; that it has nothing to do with submitting to the will of another, and everything to do with opening my inner doors so that I may know the truth of who I am.

I wonder how I will be able to maintain that sense of inner surrender in my life outside the protected walls of the meditation center.

On the afternoon of the eighth day my wandering mind composes a letter to my recently ex'd husband:

Two years ago I left you. I physically walked out the door. But never have I left you otherwise. I have carried you everywhere with me. I brought you here to India like an extra piece of heavy baggage.

I continued clinging to the illusion that we could achieve some harmony together. I remained attached to an idea of our relationship which I could not, would not, part from. I am filled with guilt over the lies I told and the unhappiness I brought to your life. I am angry that it was never acceptable for me to be angry. And I fear that you think badly of me. So you see, I have never been able to really leave you, and it causes me much pain to keep dragging you around.

I have thought about checking you for a while at the 'left luggage' counter, and picking you up on the way home. Perhaps then I will have gained the strength to carry you, and the burden won't feel so heavy. But I know that's the wrong answer.

What I want to do is simply dump some of the junk out along the way, like the guilt and the resentment and the craving and the attachment and the fear. Then I can bring home only what remains - the love I feel for you.

That's the gift I would like to give you when I return - the gift of pure love. I will ask for nothing in return, and you will be skeptical, I know. Still, I hope you will be able to accept it. There will be no more unwanted gifts from me to hide in the closets of your mind.

I know that the letter will never be sent, but it shows me a perfect example of the contents of the larger garbage heap which I drag with me everywhere. Here is one situation in my life that I am able to see where the emotional refuse comes from. Perhaps if I can get rid of this batch, I will start to make a dent in the rest of it.

I also realize that this "spiritual adventure," the search for the "Self," the quest for the Truth, is motivated by a buried knowledge which is finally rising to the surface: the fact that I have lived much of my life as a lie, and the false belief that I had no other choice but to be dishonest.

Raised by a woman who had children because "that's just what you did in those days," I was third on the scene several years after my two older brothers. The precious baby girl. Dressed like a doll and shuttled to singing and dancing lessons, my hair was peroxided blonde at age 5 and curled to look like Shirley Temple. The way my mother wished I looked.

No matter that my external presence did not reflect the truth of what I might be feeling inside. More important that I act cheek-pinching sweet and overjoyed to show off my youthful talents. Those were the things that would bring praise to my mother. "What a darling little girl you have. A real *shayna madel.*" If only her admirers knew that I emerged from my room each day with a personality to fit the occasion; a false front, one that would be acceptable, lovable, pleasing to others. Pleasing to my mother.

It was a clever deception, let down only when I returned to my room and closed the door with a sigh of relief. There I would retreat to my books, my dolls, my fantasies. Sometimes I would cry for hours, alone and afraid of being found out. For if I risked being truly myself, would anyone love me?

Will you love me, Mommy?

But, hey, everyone has their story, every family has their stuff. I had a pretty good life and wasn't abused. Just endlessly criticized, whittled away at, until there wasn't much left of the "real" me.

Like most of us do, I became a complex character in my own personal theatre of life. It was a pretty good act, too, until the curtain came crashing down unexpectedly and I found myself on the stage alone.

The final scene took place in Lake Tahoe when I was thirty years old. A gnawing restlessness and inner emptiness had driven me away from the people who cared about me and steered me off the marriage track into the "fast lane." Partying on the beach all day and dealing blackjack in a casino all night left little time for rest. But who needed rest? I needed only to numb a dull, amorphous ache and escape the feeling that I had failed miserably by not meeting others' expectations of me.

I soon discovered what I came to call my "mental pain killers." There were blue pills to help me sleep, white ones to wake me up, and a seductive crystalline powder to smooth the harsh edges of my reality and enhance my sense of personal power. Cocaine. My wonder drug. Until one night, deep into my dependency, my little vial of magic powder was empty and my sources for the drug were dry.

I began to pace the room, slowly at first, and then more and more frantically. Breath raspy, head pounding, nose running, I clutched that little glass bottle tightly in my fist until my hand cramped. Then, in a fit of rage, screamed and threw it across the room, shattering a picture frame and sending shards of glass in every direction.

The crash stopped me in my tracks. Shocked by my desperation and my extreme reaction, I sank to the floor in despair. Teetering at the edge of a bottomless well, I wondered if I could live without cocaine, if I was addicted.

The thought was humiliating. The possibility horrifying.

I finally forced myself to get up and wash my face; but when I looked in the mirror, I cringed from the misery reflected there. The emotional crisis was etched in the deep lines around my mouth, the hollows beneath my cheekbones. On the thickness of my tongue I could still taste the anxiety, the anger, the dismay, the shame. My swollen, bloodshot eyes stared back at me with the frozen fear of a doe in the path of an oncoming truck.

Looking at myself, what had become of myself, I understood that fear had the potential to either paralyze or motivate me. I decided I was already crippled enough.

I packed my bags and left town.

Living alone in Napa several months later, I saw that I could make new choices about my life; that I didn't have to continue to live it the way I had learned. So I chose instead to honor the self which I had denied – the self that felt "not good enough" just as she was and that had become the actress.

Through yoga, study and solitude, I breathed life into parts of myself which I had thought dead, and I began to listen to the voice within. It prepared me for this journey of trans-formation; guided me toward the demise of the false self.

Take it to India, and throw it on the funeral pyre.

This will undoubtedly be a long process, allowing the layers to burn away. I know there will not be a spontaneous emergence of a new "me." Only a simultaneous erosion and evolution. A continual series of mini-deaths and re-births. A person who is constantly changing; in each moment as new, different and as impermanent as she was in the last moment.

Being, becoming. Being, becoming. *Anicca, anicca, anicca.*

After tea break on the ninth day, something clicks into place. Whatever I am doing, it is working. It feels right. I finally understand why this is called meditation "practice": it takes a heck of a lot of practice to develop any skill.

While at times it is almost pleasurable to observe the subtle vibrations in my body, more often than not the sensations are painful, especially when the fire in my knees flares up or my mental ramblings hit an emotional hot spot. But the more I practice, the more I know that if I remain calm and non-reactive, a time comes when there is balance. When I am balanced. When I can watch my breath, or my sensations, or my pain, and just watch. No thought. No judgment. No craving. No aversion. No reaction at all. These are moments of liberation. These are moments of peace.

"The ninth day is over. Tomorrow this *Dhamma* seminar will come to a close." Goenka talks about how to make use of the technique we have learned here in our daily life. Otherwise the ten days becomes just another "experience" or another intellectual exercise.

He explains that any negativity that arises in the mind creates disharmony within. "How can you be angry and be happy at the same time?"

I can't. If I hold in my anger, it burns inside me and I become hostile. On the other hand, if I lose control and vent my anger, I often act in ways I am sorry for later.

"Neither suppressing anger nor giving it free license is the solution. There is a middle path. If anger has arisen, just observe the anger, without reacting. In this way you are not suppressing it, nor are you allowing it to overwhelm you.

Observing the anger, or the fear, or the craving, will eradicate the negativity and allow it to pass away."

How on earth am I supposed to 'observe' anger or fear, or anything like that? It's a feeling, an emotion, not something outside myself.

"When a negativity arises at the mental level, two biochemical changes start happening at the physical level simultaneously. The breath loses its normality, becoming erratic. At the same time, some sensation will start in the body, such as heat or tension. It is difficult to observe abstract anger or hatred or fear. So whenever a negativity arises, observe the respiration and the sensations in your body."

Bells and whistles. I get it. This is what I have been learning how to do. When I practice meditation, I strengthen my ability to observe my respiration and my sensations with a calm mind, so that I can do it when I really need to.

"If previously, out of ten times you reacted blindly every time, now maybe it will only be nine times out of ten. If one of those times the mind is balanced, instead of reacting you will observe. Just for a few moments, like a shock absorber. Reaction is always negative. Action is always positive, creative."

It seems like my whole life has been lived in reaction to someone or something outside of myself. And it is clear that the reactions have been the seeds for all the crab grass I've planted in my life, keeping me entangled to the point of strangulation.

"We always look outside ourselves for the cause of our misery. Finding fault, placing blame somewhere outside the self. Our efforts are directed at trying to change things and people outside ourselves instead of looking within to see the totality – to see the reality from different angles. Only then will we stop blaming others and accept full responsibility for our

109

misery. No one else is responsible for my misery. I am 100% responsible for my own misery."

I've already figured that one out for myself, thank you.

"We can measure our progress by the decreased length of time our misery lasts. If we used to stay mad or depressed for one year, it will soon become one month, one week, and finally one moment!"

That's the most encouraging thing I've heard yet.

"Get finely tuned by practice to your own bodily signals. Maintain awareness of *Anicca*. Changing. Impermanence. Observe the physical phenomena with equanimity. Meditation does not promote inaction. It is to train the mind to come out of the habit of blind reaction, and then to take action.

"Sometimes the action you choose may have to be 'hard line' and may even look like anger to others, but it is the motivation behind the action which is important. If you yell at a child out of your own anger, your own impure mind, it is a negative reaction. But if shouting or restraining the child is the only way to keep him from running into the street, then you take this harsh action, but always with the basis of love and compassion."

Near the end of the discourse, Goenka talks about love as a commercial business. About how when we "love" someone we expect something in return. And when we don't get it, the "love" is gone.

"This proves that I love only myself, no one else," he says. "Every relationship is to see that my desires are fulfilled. So long as that happens, I love him. When he starts doing something against my dreams, I no longer love him. I only love my dreams, myself."

A question that had come to my mind earlier in the course, about how we should go about choosing a partner if we only love ourselves, surfaces again. I decide to ask him the question later, if the opportunity arises.

Goenka's eyes are heavy. I think he looks tired. He too has been working diligently for all these days, teaching constantly, giving long talks at night, answering question after question. His voice slows finally.

"Wisdom is looking at the totality — all sides, not just external, but internal as well — to find truth, the *Dhamma*, the reality as it actually exists, not just as it appears to be. The seed of *Dhamma* you have gotten is so valuable. Preserve it and multiply."

His eyes close. "May everyone enjoy real happiness, real peace. Get liberated from the bondages of negativities, of impurities. May all beings be happy . . be happy . . be happy."

Sadhu. Sadhu. Sadhu. Well said. Well said. Well said.

Immediately, students line up to ask questions. Tired or not, Goenka smiles at each one, beckoning them forward. Finally, it is my turn.

I kneel before the Teacher. "If the ideal is pure and unconditional love for all beings, and not the care and feeding of the individual ego, how do you go about choosing a mate? Will just anybody out there do?"

He laughs gently, his belly jiggling. "No, no, no. Of course not. You will want to choose someone with good qualities of kindness, generosity, tolerance and compassion. Someone with whom you have things in common, and who shares your commitment to a life of *Dhamma.*"

That brings another question to my mind.

111

"Speaking of commitment, how can one become committed to anything or anyone knowing that it is all *anicca*, impermanent, and will change anyway?"

"My dear *Dhamma* daughter," he says kindly, raising both hands slightly. "On this hand we have the apparent reality, and on this hand we have the ultimate reality, the Truth. You must still live a life, a normal life. You must make plans, goals and commitments in your life. But to live a happy life, you follow the plans without craving and without attachment to the outcome. You accept whatever results you get with equanimity. You always do your best, keeping the mind pure from negativity. In this way, on one hand, you live a good life, a committed life, but always with the awareness of the other hand, the ultimate reality, *anicca,* this will also change."

"Be happy," he concludes. "Be happy."

On the tenth morning of the course, we learn one more meditation technique called *Metta-Bhavana*, Meditation of Loving-Kindness.

Goenka-ji explains. "When we remove our negativities and purify our minds by the practice of *Vipassana* we can finally emerge from the prison of self-obsession and begin to be truly concerned with the welfare of others. The more our inner serenity develops, the more clearly we can see how others are suffering, and the more we will develop compassion for others. *Metta* meditation is a way to share with all others the peace and harmony that we have discovered."

Even as he describes the reason for the technique, the feeling in the hall becomes soft. I feel the whole room relax. Vibrations of *Metta* swirl around the room and surround me with an aura of love and compassion. And then he begins to chant, deeply and slowly . . . ever so slowly.

"May I be freeeeeee . . . ."

The word hangs long in the air.

"May I be free from anger, hatred, animosity, ill will.

May I develop love, compassion, peace and good will.

May all beings be free from anger, hatred, animosity and ill will.

May all beings develop love, compassion, peace and good will.

May ALL beings be liberated from their suffering.

May ALL beings be happy . . be happy . . be happy."

My body swells with tears. They move upward from my heart to catch in my throat and finally spill out of my eyes.

But they are not tears of sadness, or grief, or pain. They are tears of gratitude. Tears of love. The purest love I have ever known.

I hear sniffles beside me and behind me. Noses are being blown. Practically everyone in the hall is crying. The power of *Metta* feels like a healing force being transmitted through the clear being of Goenka to all of us and all beings everywhere.

All the negativity, irritation and anger of the last ten days are washed away.

Any residue of skepticism has vanished.

The noble silence is over. So is the air of calmness and concentration that accompanied it.

I sit on my cushion for a long time, savoring the feeling in the hall. People are outside talking now, rushing to make up for so many days of lost words.

I don't even want to begin talking. Who would I talk to anyway? I feel very lonely. Strange, with all this love in the air.

I also don't look forward to the prospect of continuing the journey, alone. I want to be with someone. Someone who understands all that I have just experienced. Someone to help me sort it all out.

How long happy?

Aversion, craving, changing, changing.

Anicca, anicca, anicca.

*While I thought I was learning how to live,
I have been learning how to die.*

Leonardo Da Vinci

"Your Self is Running to Get Home"

Leaving the meditation hall on the final day, I shield my eyes from the late morning sun and look at the small crowd gathered outside, talking softly. Bright sunlight bounces off golden threads woven into an emerald green sari, and shines through the thin sleeve of a bleached white cotton shirt.

Now that the course is over, I feel some sadness and regret. I find myself wishing that I had slept less and meditated more. If only I had known in the beginning how valuable the moments here were to be; if only I had realized in the middle how quickly the days would be over. Still, I have absorbed so much. Now I need time to digest it all.

I turn at the sound of a woman's British accent. There is Anne. I have not seen her since the day of my arrival at *Dhammagiri*. How alone I have been.

"Well," she says, approaching me, "Did you have a good course?"

A "good" course?

"It was excruciating. But I think it was worth it."

"Good!"

"Why didn't I see you during the ten days?" I ask her.

"Some of the old students meditate in individual 'cells' which line the inside of the pagoda. They are just little rooms which allow for less distraction. We also sleep in tiny huts away from the dormitories and take our meals at a different time. It all provides for more isolation and deeper concentration."

It must work. She is glowing.

"Will you be staying for the next course?" she asks.

You must be kidding.

"I need a break from this. It was a big dose for my first time. But I know I'll be back again. And I'll work harder, too."

"Have a safe journey. And remember, 'Be Happy'."

How could I forget?

In Bombay, I am welcomed back into the home of the Jahandra family for a few days before I head to South India. I answer their questions about the meditation course, but find it difficult to put ten days of philosophy and experience into words that make much sense. Sense or no sense, Rina's mother identifies herself as a truly miserable person and begs me to go to a course with her so she can become liberated from her suffering. I encourage her to go herself because there are many other things I want to do in India now.

First on my agenda is to visit the *Bidi Walla Baba*, Sri Nisargadatta Maharaj, an 85 year old guru in Bombay whom I have read and heard about.

As the story goes, many years ago he was a *bidi walla*, a seller of Indian hand-made cigarettes. While taking care of business at his small *bidi* shop, Maharaj would share with customers and friends the wisdom he had gained through his self-realization of the "Ultimate Truth." Over time the word spread, and small crowds began to gather around the shop to listen.

He eventually retired from the *bidi* business, but people kept coming to hear him, and he continued to be known as the *Bidi Walla Baba*.

A lengthy taxi ride, made longer still by an emaciated strolling bovine that demands the right of way and gets it, delivers me to a plain house in an old neighborhood of the city. Upstairs is a small loft, hazy with incense and jammed with Indian disciples sitting cross-legged on the floor. The old man around whom they gather wears white cotton short-sleeved pajamas, a quarter-inch crew cut and a three-day stubble. His lips are flaccid, as if there are no teeth inside his mouth. The center of his sepia forehead is punctuated with a smear of red paste.

As I reach the top of the stairs he motions me forward with a bony arm and indicates that I should sit down in front of him. Looking directly at me with his watery eyes, he begins to speak. The Marathi dialect is gibberish to my ears.

A man sitting closely to his left translates the words in English.

"Your Self is running to get home."

I glance around in discomfort at being the center of attention, wondering how this skinny old man could look at me so intensely for a moment and tell me in a language I don't even understand the truest thing I have ever heard about myself.

The flow of strange words begins again, and the other man continues to translate.

"From where have you come?"

"America," I reply.

The guru looks at the burning stick of incense he holds in his hand and grunts.

"Do you have any family?"

"Yes. I have a mother and a father, and two brothers and their families."

"No children?"

"No children."

Grunt.

"What have you been doing here in India?"

"I have been learning *Vipassana* meditation from Sri Goenka at Igatpuri."

He listens to this information through the interpreter, and nods with recognition at the name of my meditation teacher.

He lights another stick of incense and puts it into the holder before him, which holds several burning sticks already and is covered with ashes.

After observing me quietly for a moment more, he grunts a few more times and indicates that I can stay.

I move back and take a place on the crowded floor among the numerous Indian devotees.

The guru begins to speak, pausing to light more incense and smack his floppy lips while the interpreter translates.

"Mind and intellect are incapable of understanding who you really are. They are only obstacles to understanding. Once true knowledge dawns, mind and intellect become inoperative."

He watches the smoke curling from the row of joss sticks.

"Consciousness becomes like a telescope through which you see life manifestation, but this is not the primary principle of consciousness. One must get rid of the body state. I am this. I am one with this manifestation. I am consciousness."

It doesn't make much sense to me, but still I find myself getting pulled in.

"Whatever we accept as truth from mind and intellect cannot stay. It is always changing. Start observing the state of this consciousness in the formless state."

Wait a minute. This sounds like what I have been learning.

The sound of footsteps coming up the stairs interrupts him. A western man, tall, clean-cut, maybe late twenties, enters the loft.

Maharaj looks at him, lights some more incense, and proceeds to give him the third degree.

"Where have you come from, what have you been doing in India, and what is your purpose for being *here?*"

Obviously the old man thinks young westerners are just interested in adding a "guru" to their list of things to see in India, and that we are not really seekers of Truth. He might be right; but he certainly doesn't give the new visitor any breaks.

The fellow becomes flustered, but does his best to appear sincere. My heart goes out to him, but I also feel like laughing. *Who is this old guy anyway, and why is he putting us on the spot?*

Although I haven't used it much myself, I feel the need to transmit an important piece of advice I received before beginning this journey.

Leaning forward, I say very quietly, "keep a sense of humor." The young man turns to look at me, and smiles. The old man lights some incense, grunts, flaps his lips and says he can stay.

The esoteric monologue resumes.

"Your consciousness creates the characters and other lives of your dreams."

Someone poses a question. "Maharaj, is the consciousness real or unreal?"

Maharaj answers, "It is a dreaming consciousness. You are unreal, therefore the world is unreal. When you have all the knowledge you realize all the world is illusion."

There it is again. Anicca.

He closes his eyes for a moment, grunts and finally puts the incense down. Dark heads touch the floor and people begin to rise. I am glad it is over. My head is swimming with sandalwood smoke and confusion.

A large woman approaches me. Her generous stomach hangs over the waist of her brocade sari and her eyes are outlined with dark *kohl*. A slash of red color defines the part in her heavily oiled black hair, identifying her as a married woman. A crimson paper circle the size of a dime is stuck on the center of her forehead.

"You are coming with us?" She speaks in a clipped Indian English accent. "Today is a special day. It is the anniversary of the passing from this life of Maharaj's guru. We are proceeding to the gravesite for *bhajan*. It is a devotional worship. You must be coming along."

As she speaks, her head seems to wobble back and forth gently on her neck. I wonder if the incense has gone to my brain, but no. Her head is definitely swaying from side to side.

I feel a hand on my elbow and turn to see a broad smile on the face of the young western man. "I'm David, from San Diego," he says in a distinctly American voice. "Shall we go together?"

The woman chimes in. "You will be coming with us in our cars. Just meet down in front."

"Thank you," David and I say simultaneously.

"It is nothing," she says, smiling. Her head sways from side to side again, and my own head feels loose upon my neck just watching her.

We all pile into the waiting automobiles, which caravan through narrow congested streets to a broad avenue and then to the edge of the city overlooking the waters of the Arabian Sea. When we arrive at the site, we find Maharaj with a garland of orange flowers around his neck and another around his head. He chants a *mantra* as he sprinkles water and throws petals on the shrine of his own guru. The other devotees begin to sing, and soon the mood becomes one of festivity.

Plates of food appear. There are *samosas*, the delicious fried triangles stuffed with vegetables, and rice balls, and oranges.

A man comes by with a bowl of deep red powder, dips in his fingertip and puts a *tika* mark in the center of my forehead. He tells me the dot symbolizes the "third eye," the eye with which we see psychically.

I smile and thank him. His head sways from side to side.

I quietly ask David if he knows what it means when someone moves their head around loosely.

"It seems to be a gesture of affirmation in India, meaning 'yes' or 'no problem' or 'I understand.' Does that answer your question?"

I move my head awkwardly from side to side.

Afterward, David and I, our red *tikas* smearing quickly in the heat of the day, walk back through overflowing neighborhoods to the central part of the city, stopping for

123

fresh coconut slices at the stand of a street vendor.

We talk non-stop and become friends very quickly. Whether it is the camaraderie of finding a fellow Californian on the other side of the world or our common pursuit of spiritual understanding, it is an open, honest and warm relationship right from the start. We agree to meet again the following day at the loft of Maharaj.

The small room is crowded again. David and I squeeze into a corner. The guru keeps lighting sticks of incense until I think I will suffocate.

"What is that state in which there is no 'I' and no 'you'? Nothing is there, only that is the eternal truth. What is your real nature? How do you identify yourself? If you identify with the body, along with the body you will die."

He speaks in fits and starts, sometimes dispassionately, sometimes accusingly.

"I do not want to teach anything to anybody. I only hold up a spiritual mirror to those who come here. You have to get the vision of yourself in the light that is emanating from your own Self."

The curling wisps of smoke make me feel dizzy. My stomach begins to cramp up and I have an urgent need to go to the bathroom.

"If you say that you have understood, you have not understood. Whatever you have tried to understand during your spiritual search will prove false. Therefore nothing is to be understood. Deliberate on this."

It is then that my insides decide to come out, and I run down the narrow stairs to find a toilet.

As I squat there in the dim light, I wonder who decides that someone is a prophet, an enlightened being. Were we all just falling for some bad joke up there? While I think I understand some of what the old man said, according to him if I think I understand anything I have missed the point.

Maybe it will all become clear to me one day, but right now it isn't any clearer than the wispy haze of incense which fills the Bidi Walla Baba's loft.

Clutching my stomach, I finally stumble out to see David's concerned face. He helps me get a taxi to Rina's apartment.

The glare from the light bulb hanging over my bed is reflected in her father's glasses so that I cannot see any eyes, just orbs of light. Mr. Jahandra reprimands me gently for eating at a street stall and gives me some large white pills to swallow. I am experiencing my first bout with dysentery, accompanied by a fever of 102 F. In between trips to the bathroom I remind myself that it's only temporary. "*Anicca, anicca, anicca.*"

The next morning my fever is down and my stomach cramps are gone.

No more eating on street corners for me.

I walk over to the coffee shop at the Taj Majal Hotel and order a yogurt *lassi*. Sipping the cool drink, I try to gather my strength for the journey ahead. Tomorrow I depart by steamship down the coast to the beaches of Goa and southward. There's only one hitch:

I don't want to carry my jeans and boots which I packed for the mountains of Nepal with me to the sweltering south of India, but I don't want to have to come back to Bombay again, either. Do I leave my extra things at Rina's or take them with me?

125

I feel irritated by either choice, and generally unsatisfied about what to do. Meditating would probably help me out, but I am too agitated to sit. I begin to think I wasted my time at the course for ten days.

Maybe the *Bidi Walla Baba* was right. As I hurriedly left the loft I heard him call after me, "Without continuing awareness all that you have gained could be lost. . ."

There at the lunch counter, half-empty glass of *lassi* in my hand, white paper napkin on my lap, I notice for a moment that my breath is coming in and going out. I am aware of the weight of the glass in my hand, the pressure of my back against the chair, the quiet play of vibrations throughout my body.

I decide to leave my extra bag behind and travel lightly.

If the doors of perception were cleansed.
Everything would appear as it is, infinite.

William Blake

Promise to Remember Me

David surprises me at the steamship dock at 8:00 a.m. to wish me *bon voyage*. We both agree how nice it would be for him to come along to the beaches of Goa with me; but he already has reservations north and is looking forward to getting back to the States next week. We have only just met, but we shared so much about our personal and spiritual journeys that he feels like a long-time friend. Our parting is bittersweet.

Shortly after departure, I look for a place to settle myself on the deck of the weather beaten steamer, and wonder if I've boarded a throbbing, swaying sea monster by mistake. The disorienting loss of equilibrium that usually keeps me off boats keeps me close to the rail for a dose of ocean breeze. It will be a long, overnight voyage down the west coast of India. A good chance to "just observe" the feeling of physical imbalance with a balanced mind.

Looking around at the other passengers talking together or sharing a meal, I feel acutely the isolation of the lone traveler and wish I had a companion on the ride; not even someone to talk to, but just to be with. People express surprise, especially the locals, that I am alone on this vessel. They eye me with curiosity. But their sideways looks don't bother me. The many times I have eaten in restaurants by myself or gone to the movies alone has made the solitary "image" an easy one to wear. It's the actuality that isn't always enjoyable.

The monotonous swaying and throbbing and vibrating begin to fill me with agitation. When I close my eyes to meditate I get dizzy and nauseous. I finally give up and go down below to find an empty bunk for the night. But being on the lower level makes me feel even worse. Deciding that the fresh air is a better choice, I spread my cotton blanket down on the hard wooden deck to sleep. But there is no sleep. Only my mind, playing its repetitive refrain.

I hate this boat. I want off this boat more than anything in the world. I want to get to the Himalayas, to stand on top of a mountain. It feels like this voyage will never end. I wish I could sleep.

Always craving, always aversion, always *anicca, anicca, anicca.*

I finally doze off, awakening to the colors of sunrise and the smell of *chai.*

Upon my arrival at the port of Goa, I decide to take a morning bus tour through the capital city of Panjim. A young Indian woman with a shy smile and soft brown doe eyes is the tour guide. A jet black braid hangs down to her waist. She wears loose cotton pants and a matching print top which reaches to her knees. A long silky scarf billows around her neck as the breeze blows in through the coach windows.

Gita introduces herself as a college student. She explains that Goa was a Portuguese enclave for 450 years, but that India finally ejected the Portuguese in 1961.

The imposing cathedrals and the red tile roofs of the charming "old city" retain the flavor of Portugal. It provides an unusual background for women bustling by in flowing saris and street vendors selling day-glo pictures of Hindu gods and goddesses.

As we wander through the streets of Old Goa, Gita tells me that her job pays for her tuition and helps to support her family. At the end of the tour she approaches me, and takes my left hand in both of hers. Her fingers are long and cool.

"You know," she says, "I would very much like to have a watch like this."

I look down at my Timex. It is the first watch I have worn in years, purchased especially for the journey to help me make trains on time. It is not expensive. I feel secure with it wrapped snugly around my wrist. I am not ready to give it up.

Explaining apologetically that I need my watch, I thank her for being an excellent tour guide and hand her a tip of several *rupees.*

A few moments later she is beside me again, her sad eyes looking even more hopeless. Suddenly she presses a piece of paper into my hand on which she has scrawled her address.

"Please send me a watch like this from your country," she says desperately, squeezing my hand. "Please do not forget me. Promise to remember me."

I don't know what to say. I nod silently and put the paper in my pocket. As I walk away down the palm shaded street, I hear her softly plead once more. The despair in her voice pulls at my heart.

"Promise to remember me."

The grass is always greener where I'm not.

I sit on my patio outside my room in Colva Beach and watch an incredible orange ball of a sun set over a picturesque, palm lined beach in one of the most exotic places on earth. And all I want to do is go home.

I'm at the Tourist Bungalow, but there aren't many tourists around. Only a bunch of unkempt long-haired European vagabonds, traveling "on the cheap," camping out and smoking dope on the long curving stretch of fine sand. It looks like a scene right out of the sixties. But I rarely feel like I'm in the right place or time zone anyway. Seems like I'm always running to catch up, to be "in." To feel part of something.

Even while married, I felt so isolated, so alone, so disconnected. That's why I ended up leaving. Both times. With someone else. Nobody's fault but my own. Just spreading my misery around, looking for something or someone to make me happy. It worked for a little while. But Goenka is right. "How long happy?" How long before the next craving sets in?

I realize that there hasn't been a real thread, a true bond, probably since I was in the womb. Once the cord was cut, I was on my own. I feel like I have spent my whole life looking for someone to hold me when I cry. I long for a place of warmth and safety where I can just be myself.

I close my eyes and meditate, concentrating on my breath, on my sensations, the subtle vibrations, with awareness. Ahhh. Here is the place where I am myself, at least for the moment.

I wait for the early morning bus to take me away from Colva, deeper into the heart of India. Shopkeepers sweep their entrances, but the dirt just moves from one place to another, leaving a fine layer of dust everywhere. It seems impossible to keep things clean in India.

The streets are stained with splashes of what looks like dark blood. A lot of Indian people chew *pan*, a combination of broken-up chunks of betel nut, some ground spices and a dab of lime, all rolled up in a betel leaf and stuck in the mouth. It turns their mouths and lips blood red and they spit long streams of crimson juice everywhere.

A dilapidated bus finally arrives. Three hours later it breaks down at the Karwar depot. As I wait for it to be repaired, I look around and realize that nothing I see fits into the frame of my own life's experiences. Dirty, sweaty, barefoot people overflow every bench and fill every corner. Flies alight on the drool of babies. A wild-eyed holy man in a loincloth with matted hair talks to himself. A boy with twisted legs slithers along the grimy floor. Packs of stray dogs with hairless patches of oozing skin fight over scraps of paper with barely a lick of food on them.

Sticky heat saps the last ounce of energy from my body. A bottle of warm lemon soda is the only option to wet my parched throat, and I can stomach only one sip of the sweet liquid. The "ladies' room" is revolting, with urine and feces spread all over the floor. Still, I stand there and pee among the shit and stink and bugs, hardly phased at all.

Is this "equanimity" or stupidity?

Arriving at last in Mangalore for an overnight rest before continuing south, I throw my duffle down beside the bed in a cheap, stuffy hotel room and open the window. Along with a rush of hot air comes in a flurry of mosquitoes. I hurriedly close the window and sink down onto the mattress, depressed. It is a familiar feeling, like a blanket of darkness blocking out the source of light. I think I am homesick.

A question repeats itself over and over in my mind, whether my eyes are open to my surroundings, or closed in frustrated attempts at meditation:

What am I doing here? Alone?

Other people's judgments about this journey leave me confused. Travelers that I meet along the way say to me, "You're so brave. I really admire you."

I'm not sure it's courage at all, but rather cowardice. For me it's easier to run away to some other part of the world than to have to make decisions about the rest of my life. Running away has always been my first choice. I see now how this way of reacting has not solved anything.

I decide that I have made a terrible mistake by coming to India and am filled with regrets about my decision to travel instead of continuing my education. I wonder how my time here could possibly equal in value what I would be learning at home? I worry about how I will be able to support myself and go to school when I get back. My thoughts spiral around and around in my head until it begins to ache.

And then I notice the ache. The intensity of the sensation. It reminds me to be aware, to be equanimous. As I continue to observe the pain in my head, my breath coming in and going out, the different sensations throughout my body, my thoughts start to calm down – a little.

Oh, it is only my wild mind, always rolling in the past, worrying about the future. My work is to be here now and accept the reality "as it is." This storm will pass. Like everything else, it is anicca.

134

The ceiling fan spins overhead in unending circles. I identify with its circuitous pattern, for even though I have changed my external environment I cannot escape the punkah fan of my mind, constantly whirling round and round.

I begin to understand that the journey itself cannot change me. Only I can change me. I suppose that could happen here, there or anywhere. It's less about where I go, and more about who I am.

The most foreign country is within.

Alice Walker

From the Inside Out

Deep in the heart of South India, the train from Mangalore to Cochin is filled to overflowing. I am one of four people pressed tightly together on a seat made for three. My clothes are layered with Indian dust, my body is sticky from tropical heat, and I long for a drink of cool, pure water. I feel irritated that I have wasted so much of my time in India standing in ticket lines, waiting in crowded depots and being crammed into second-class rail cars. I just want to get where I'm going.

The train stops briefly at a local station. Food vendors and *chai wallahs* hawk their wares on the steamy station platform while pathetic children and deformed beggars reach claw-like hands through open coach windows. Some people give them money. Others ignore them or shoo them away.

An adolescent girl appears in the half-open window near me, her classic Asian beauty undiminished by her ragged clothing. Pressing her palms flat against the grimy glass, she looks at me. Gazes deeply into my eyes. Silently reaches into my heart and asks for mercy. Suddenly, all the irritation I feel is washed away by a river of compassion, and a flood of helplessness.

If only I had the power . . . but nothing I can give you will change your life.

I reach into my bag and hand her a banana. She looks disappointed, but takes the fruit with both hands and touches it to her forehead in thanks. Then she disappears.

An emaciated cow sticks her nose through the vacated window. Receiving no offering, she turns around, raises her tail and relieves herself on the rails before strolling away.

With a shrill whistle blast, the train pulls out of the station and rolls into the vastness of the Indian countryside. An elderly *sadhu* in orange robes walks through the coach chanting words of Hindu scripture. My neighbor, a middle-aged gentleman in a turban, translates what the holy man is saying: "From the nameless I get thousands of names; from the formless I get millions of forms."

A little girl across the aisle taps me on the arm and shyly offers me an orange from her mother's basket. I look over at the mother. Behind the veil of her thin cotton *sari,* a wisp of a smile floats over her solemn face. Taking the fruit with both hands, I touch it to my forehead in thanks.

Zzzzzzzzzttt!

The touch of the orange on my skin is like an electric shock, and I am bolted into awareness. In that moment, instead of feeling like I'm wasting time being on the road, it becomes perfectly clear that *being on the road is where it's at.*

I suddenly understand that traveling on my own in India is not about seeing a particular sight and then getting to the next place to see what's there. It's about the *process* of moving from place to place: the interactions with people along the way; the passing scenes from a life so foreign to my own; the poverty, the generosity, the misery, the inner strength.

It's about accepting whatever each moment offers, exactly as it is, with equanimity – and gratitude.

Traveling in India becomes a metaphor for living my life, as I realize that the journey itself is the ultimate destination.

And though I am truly sick of the smell of cow pee, the taste of Limca soda and the stickiness of my own body, I feel a smile slowly spreading throughout my being.

There is nowhere in the world I would rather be than crammed into this second-class rail car deep in the heart of South India right now.

Finally accepting that the grass is green enough exactly where I am, I am also able to accept something about myself which I thought must be a character deficiency, especially for a traveler.

The truth is, I have little interest in statistics or history.

It matters not to me how many people populate a particular town or city, but whether the residents are sensitive or rude, joyful or reserved, curious or aloof, trustworthy or dishonest.

More important to me than who built an ancient structure in what bygone year is how it feels to be there, to touch the stone which gives it form, to watch the patterns of changing light on its surfaces, to understand its place in people's lives.

And, this one feels like heresy, historical museums with their relics of the past tucked away behind glass bore me. History is being created anew in every passing moment; and I want to experience it as it happens, not look back upon it.

It is *life* which fascinates me with its unfolding, *art* which touches the depths of my soul, *nature* which connects me to every living thing, *humanity* which reveals to me the spirit of the divine.

So with a sigh of relief and a sense of appreciation for who I *am*, instead of guilt about who I think I *should* be, I forgive myself for not caring about information which does not interest me. I will simply *be* here, seeing, hearing, tasting, smelling, touching and feeling with my heart.

Traveling from the inside out.

All journeys have secret destinations
of which the traveler is unaware.

Martin Buber

The Backwaters of Kerala

I sit at the edge of the Bay of Cochin, watching a little fish skim along the top of the water, gathering a meal of floating bugs. Then he plunges beneath the surface, only to reappear in a moment and repeat the performance. I have never seen anything like it. The show keeps me entranced while I wait for the clerk from the Bolgatty Hotel to determine if there is space for me tonight.

It turns out that the historic hotel is indeed full, but I am told "Not to worry, madam. We will arrange accommodation for you." A moment later a young boy with a shock of black hair appears and is given instructions in the local dialect by the clerk, who then turns to me. "Please, madam. The boy will be taking you. Please follow along with him."

I am escorted down the road to the modest home of a family living nearby. Two children peek out from behind the folds of their mother's *sari* as the father greets me outside. "We are having a room for you in our house. Only ten *rupees.*

145

Would you like to see?"

The children run to open the front door for me and I step into a large, plain room with concrete walls and floor, a single bed and a small table and chair. "The toilet room is down the hall and we will give dinner at six o'clock."

I realize that I am standing in what is meant to be the living room of the house, and that this room no doubt provides a goodly portion of their income. The look of nervous anticipation in the eyes of each member of the family turns to the joy of relief when I say "okay." The man calls to the boy who brought me and hands him some coins, then he and his wife disappear into the house.

The family's two children stand in the doorway and silently scrutinize my every move as I lay some things out on the bed and wash up in a bowl of warm water which has been put on the table. It is obvious they are not going away.

"What is your name?" I ask the girl, who appears to be about five and is the older of the two.

"My name is Mallika. This is my brother Jai." Little Jai's black eyes are wide with wonder as he points at my toothbrush and toothpaste.

Soon the parents come in from the kitchen with a large plate of rice, *dal* and *chapatis*. Again, the whole family waits with expectant anticipation. I tear off a piece of *chapati*, use it to scoop up some of the rice and *dal*, and put the whole thing into my mouth. They watch me chew. They watch me swallow. I am the only show in town.

I tell them the food is delicious. The parents nod and smile and leave the room, herding the children out with them. For a few minutes I am alone. Privacy, that precious

146

commodity in India. But it doesn't last long. The children are soon back, watchful as ever. The toilet becomes my only refuge. Even then the children wait outside the door until I come out and follow me back to my room, continuing to look at me as if I am from another planet.

There's certainly no doubt that I'm from another world.

The next afternoon, while touring Cochin on foot, I discover that the food in the south is delightfully tasty and incredibly inexpensive. Two *rupees*, about twenty cents, buys me a *masala dosa*, a light and crispy rolled up pancake about twenty-four inches long, filled with curried vegetables and served with a spicy soup called *sambar* and a side of coconut chutney. Or for the same price I can have a *thali* plate, a combination of rice and several small bowls filled with various vegetables and condiments.

I've noticed that the people in this southernmost state of Kerala are of darker complexion, with oiled, wavy hair. They are more African looking than people farther north, especially the old women with their big elongated ear holes. I think the young women are prettier than those in Bombay, and their eyes are not so sad. Most of the men are dressed in white short-sleeved shirts and plaid *lungis,* the cotton wrap-around sarongs, which they constantly play with, flipping the cloth up and down from knee length to ankle length and back up again. It's like a regional pastime.

The buildings in Kerala are in better shape than anywhere I have been, sporting lots of fresh paint. It seems the people here generally take more pride in their surroundings and themselves. That may go hand in hand with the fact that the literacy rate is much higher in this part of the country.

My walking tour has a specific destination, and an unusual one for India: a Jewish synagogue. I had read about the "White Jews of Cochin" and one isolated Jewish community which has survived for several centuries. It is on my personal list of "must sees." I finally find it among narrow streets lined with spice traders. The air is filled with the smells of ginger, cardamom, cumin and cloves. The street signs proclaim "Jew Town Road."

The caretaker and guardian of the temple, Jackie Cohen, welcomes me graciously. His smiling face is deeply lined, and a black *yarmulke* sits rakishly on his thinning head of hair.

Jackie proudly shows me an ancient stone slab set into the wall, which is inscribed in Hebrew. He says it is from a previous temple built in 1344 that no longer exists. He also points out the blue and white hand-painted floor tiles, "no two of which are exactly alike," which had been brought from China in the eighteenth century.

As he gladly poses for my camera in front of the scrolls of the Torah, he explains that the young people of the community are all leaving, many of them to move to Israel.

"There are only about sixty of us left here," he says, "and we are all old. When we are gone that will be the end of it."

It feels good to be in the synagogue, to connect my ancestry with my present in such an unusual place. I realize that I do feel an attachment to "my" people, although I have no logical reason to. I have never studied or practiced Judaism, or given it any significance in my life. My two older brothers were Bar Mitzvahed, but no value was placed on my receiving religious training. I thought my parents were hypocrites because they were Jewish only on the holidays, or when they didn't want me to date non-Jewish boys. I often lied about my religion to other kids to avoid their discrimination or derogatory remarks. I will never forget being called a "Christ killer" at six years old, and while having no idea what that meant, feeling that I must be a horrible person.

Standing in the Cochin temple, I understand that while being Jewish has nothing to do with religion for me, it has everything to do with my cultural heritage, for which I have a deep respect. It is part of who I am.

No matter what other philosophies or practices I may adopt in my life, nothing will change the fact that I am Jewish. And for the first time, that is fine with me.

The next day in Cochin I board one of the motorized boats that ply a complex network of inland waterways known as the "backwaters of Kerala." Locals use the boats as public transportation between nearby towns, and the waterways seem to provide a main transportation artery throughout the state.

As I head south toward Alleppey, I see that the "commuter" boats are not the only craft on the water. Chinese long boats, their torn and patched sails flapping in the breeze, are propelled by dark, sinewy bodies pushing wooden poles along the river bottom. An occasional canoe glides by, filled to overflowing with coconuts. In some channels the surface is blanketed by a thick cover of water lilies, their leaves glowing golden in the afternoon sun.

Along the lush bank, tall palm trees rustle and flutter in the breeze as children laugh and play beneath them. Together they create sweet music and lively choreography – nature's own song and dance routine.

I take a picture of a woman lifting her child into a rowboat

149

from a small landing. She notices, but is not offended; rather, her face expresses curiosity about why in the world I would want to photograph this simple act of her daily existence.

It makes me realize that my taking pictures in the open market places which I find so fascinating, would be comparable to some foreign traveler in America taking pictures of me pushing a cart around the supermarket. I guess it's all relative.

The ride on the backwaters is my favorite experience so far; India at its best for me. The pendulum has swung again and I am feeling high. But I must not forget that "this will also change." *Anicca.* That seems important to remember when times are good, too.

Sitting next to me are a friendly couple, Ron and Rae, a young American man and an English girl who live together in Germany. It is pleasant to share the ride with them, until the fight breaks out.

Ron has lovely blond hair which hangs to his shoulders. The young, dark Indian fellows sitting behind him just cannot resist touching it. Ron waves them off a couple of times, like flies, but they continue to stroke his head.

Rae and I go on talking, but Ron becomes quiet. He is obviously irritated, and when they go on playing with his hair he turns around to give them a dirty look.

"Hey, cut it out, will you?"

"Okay, so sorry," one of the irritators says, but a moment later Ron feels his hair being touched again. I notice his jaw harden and his fists clench.

"Why don't we move to another seat?" I suggest quietly.

"Why should we?" he seethes. "We were here first, and they can bloody well keep their hands to themselves."

But they don't. And a moment later Ron blows. With fire in his eyes he jumps up from his seat, knocking Rae into me, and punches one of the Indians in the chest. The guy is so surprised, he turns and punches his friend, who strikes back at Ron. Other men decide to join in, and soon there are fists flying everywhere. It has turned into a free-for-all.

Rae's face is ashen. I feel her fingernails press deeply into my arm. Heart pounding, I lurch out of my seat and drag her with me. The Indian women aboard quickly gather the two of us protectively among them, shielding us with their *saris* and clucking to each other. At that moment, I imagine that I can understand Hindi. I am sure they are saying, "Sometimes men are such jerks."

Finally some sane men get everybody separated and calmed down, but the tension remains high for another half-hour until we dock. Rae won't even look at Ron, whose nose is bloodied and shirt torn. Ron's eyes are still narrowed and his cheek is twitching. My heart has slowed down, but my stomach is churning. I have to go to the bathroom. Badly.

When we reach Alleppey I disembark quickly, sorry to leave Rae behind but anxious to get a hotel room before darkness falls. I take the first cheap accommodation I can find. It turns out to be a horrible little room, in which I know I'll never sleep. The old adage "you get what you pay for" is true, and six *rupees* isn't much. At least there aren't any roaches or mosquitos. Nor is there any space or fresh air. But there is always room for reflection.

I take my shoes off and lie down on the bed, thinking about the events of the last hour. It is clear that aversion is as great an enemy as craving, maybe worse. To burn, to hate

151

seems to cause more suffering than anything.

Ron is handsome and intelligent, but he remains a slave to his reactions. I watched with my own eyes as he created his own misery and spread it around to everyone else.

Why is it always easier to see it in others than in myself?

I also remember and appreciate the protection of the women, and I realize that the women of India have been aware of me on other occasions, too. It may simply be a subtle eye contact or a small motion of the hand saying "come stand by us," "come sit by me;" but they let me know that they are there, that we need to take care of each other. For that, I am grateful.

It seems that I have finally, after my difficult period, become comfortable with India and her ways, able to change with India and to accept the constant changes in my own being. I also see the value in keeping my sense of humor and not taking things so very personally. No matter where I am or what is going on, my job is to just observe, without reaction, and then take whatever action is called for. My breathing and my sensations really do act as signals, and as guides. I think the equanimity factor truly is the key to happiness.

Kovalam Beach is at the southern tip of India, a unique place to watch the sun both rise and set over the ocean.

I have rented a thatched cottage on the beach for a couple of days, where I sit on the porch and watch the fishermen haul in their daily catch with huge, hand-tied nets. Occasionally I see some Indian ladies go for a swim in their *saris*. The cottages around me are primarily populated by low-budget, dope-smoking travelers from Europe. I spend most of my time alone.

Wandering through the exclusive Ashok Beach Hotel on my last morning in Kovalam, I see a sign advertising "Special Kerala Body Massages."

Now that sounds good!

At the appointed time, a stocky Indian lady takes me to another of the many thatched cottages on the beach and directs to me undress and lay on a table. There she promptly slathers me with enough coconut oil to deep fry me. She then proceeds to rub, rub, rub it into my skin, never going deep enough to come in contact with a muscle. After thirty minutes, she collects her thirty *rupees* and leaves.

I don't end up very relaxed, but I sure am smoooooth.

The afternoon bus to Trivandrum is as crowded as they come, but I am so smooth that I slide right in. The driver lets me sit on a little fold-out seat right behind him. I am surrounded by about twenty standing men who jostle each other to get a better look at me.

In order to avoid their stares, I direct my eyes to the floor of the bus and am fascinated by the pattern of many feet packed tightly together – my little swollen white ones surrounded by their wide cracked brown ones. It would make a great photograph, but I realize that trying to capture it on film would disrupt the perfection of the design. It is one of those images that I commit to memory, adding it to a growing list of "my favorite untaken photos."

Upon my arrival in Trivandrum, I go directly to the Air Lanka office and take my place in a slow-moving line to buy a plane ticket to Sri Lanka. An American woman ahead of me in line is agitated by the long wait. Her breath comes out in loud huffs of impatience and she runs her fingers through her hair as if she would pull it out by the roots. She complains loudly to her companion, then to everyone else around, and finally yells at the clerk, calling him incompetent. By this time her face is red and her mouth is distorted with anger. I can feel the heat she is generating as she burns inside, and move back a little so as not to get singed.

Seeing her irritation and short fuse reminds me of Blonde Ron on the boat, and myself, too, often times in the past. We are so adept at making ourselves miserable and spreading our misery around to anyone we come in contact with.

For the second time in two days I am grateful for the little bit of equanimity I've developed. It feels so much better to be balanced — to accept the reality as it is, knowing it will soon change, and take positive action instead of being controlled by negative reaction. After all, this line won't last forever. It probably won't even last another ten minutes. Surely I could use that time to read, or talk with someone, or, better yet, to simply be aware of my breath, aware of my sensations, aware of the truth of impermanence, *anicca*, playing itself out moment by moment, until it is my turn.

How much unhappiness I have already eliminated from my life by learning this one simple lesson! I feel as though I've finally passed first grade. I wonder what I will find at the next level?

A discovery is said to be an accident meeting a prepared mind.

Albert Szent-Gyorgyi

A Jewish Buddhist?

The ladies' *saris* in Sri Lanka look softer than those in India; more filmy, with paler colors and lighter fabrics. The people feel softer, too; less pushy and more thoughtful.

The island sits off the southeastern tip of India and was previously known as Ceylon. I discover with delight that the disquieting vibrations which disturbed me so much in the streets of India are absent in the capital city of Colombo. Perhaps it is because Sri Lanka is less crowded, less poor, less chaotic; or perhaps because I am less fearful, less angry, less reactive.

My first stop is the post office, which yields wonderful surprises from home.

Dad writes with the same silliness that peppers his conversation and makes him so lovable. "Did you come to go that time when you went? Drive slow, be careful, don't get lost. Si Si, Oui Oui, Pee Pee. Daddy love you, yes he do, xxxooo."

He is the one person who I know loves me unselfconsciously and completely, and the one who can always make me smile. My heart tugs with missing him.

My mother's words feel forced. I know that letter writing is a chore for her, and that expressing herself at all is difficult. I sense that she has made the effort because she wants to connect with me, but she doesn't know how. "I hope you are relaxing and having a good time. We are doing fine." How little she knows me. How little she has allowed me to know her.

There are two other letters from friends. A real cache. It was worth the trip over just to collect the mail. I needed to touch the familiarity of home; to have it touch me. To know that people still care.

While at the tourist office seeking accommodation, I meet three Australian travelers, Lynn and Brad, a couple, and Mick, their friend. They invite me to join them for dinner and a curbside seat at a parade scheduled for the evening.

As darkness falls over the city, the streets are filled with music and commotion. We find a spot on the crowded main road in time to see sixty elephants march by, all dressed up in brightly embroidered finery, complete with silk tassels and strings of flashing lights. Ornately costumed dancers gyrate to the forceful, rhythmic beating of drums, and fire eaters dramatically thrust huge flaming torches down their throats.

It is an exciting spectacle, and I feel like a kid at my first parade. *Come to think of it, this is my first parade.*

I realize that I am a thirty-two year old kid who has a lot of catching up to do.

Several children appear on bicycles, racing along the edge of the parade. With shouts and whoops of laughter, they zip past the elephants and dancers and fire eaters, hair flying in the wind, spirits riding free.

Watching them, a knot forms in my stomach and I recall a time in grammar school when all my friends had new bikes except me. My mother thought two-wheeling around town was too dangerous, so I was given a giant-size tricycle instead. But it couldn't keep up with the fast bikes, and my friends teased me for having a "baby trike." Anyway, I was too busy being shuttled around to dancing and singing lessons to ride bikes, and pretended not to care how much fun they were having zipping around, hair flying in the wind, spirits riding free.

I finally learned to ride a two-wheel bicycle at age twenty-three. It's a long way to fall when you're all grown up, trying to make up for lost time.

It was my father who drove me to the singing and dancing lessons, and everywhere else. My mother was afraid to learn to drive, and didn't think it necessary for me to learn either. In high school, my hands shook so badly each time I held a steering wheel that three learner's permits expired without my taking the driver's test. It seemed like everyone in high school had their license except me. What fun they had, zipping around, hair flying in the wind, spirits riding free.

It wasn't until I left home to go to college that I tried to drive again. My hands shook so badly each time I took the driver's license test that it took three tries before I received a passing score.

Riding a bike, driving a car, hiking, camping, skiing, eating Chinese food, going away to college — each time I pushed beyond a limitation or fear passed down to me by my mother, I felt her disapproval. The joy of accomplishment and of expanding my world was accompanied by guilt. Guilt about meeting my own needs, instead of hers.

But the distortion of her relationship to me was not clear until the day I called her from San Francisco to sadly announce the break-up of my first marriage, and she angrily replied, "How could you do this to me?"

To you? What does this have to do with you?

It was many years later when I told her I would travel to India and Nepal alone. When she responded with "Couldn't you please wait until after I'm dead?" she wasn't kidding. But I had put myself on hold long enough. No longer would her fears and her needs limit my life.

No, Mother. I will not wait until you are dead to be alive.

As the parade winds down, we wander to a nearby outdoor cafe for cool drinks. The Australians are pleasant company until the end of the evening when Mick, on his fourth beer, begins advancing toward me in an undesirable way. I move away, but that is too subtle for him. A moment later he is close beside me again, arm around my shoulder, face in my face.

I push him away gently. "Please, leave me alone."

My voice falls on deaf ears. His arm grasps me tighter.

A tendril of fear tickles my throat, raising the level of my voice. "I said I want to be left alone."

He looks totally surprised, as if he can't believe that I am telling the truth. His face twists into a crooked smile as his arm tightens around me again, grabbing my shoulder. His mouth comes close to my ear, the Australian accent thick.

"You can't fool me, lady. I know what you want."

Now my heart is pounding through my chest. My throat is tight, my jaw locked, my eyes narrow. And then I realize that what I am feeling is not fear, but anger.

160

I take a moment to notice the sensations of my heart, my throat, my jaw, my eyes. I force my breathing to become measured, slow and deep. And when I speak through clenched teeth, loud enough for the others to hear, he knows I'm telling the truth.

"Get the hell away from me – NOW!"

Humiliated and angry, Mick backs off and I jump out of my seat, knocking his bottle of beer onto his lap. He looks shocked, his friends look apologetic, and I just pick up my bag and stomp away.

Interesting that the only sexual aggression I have experienced on a journey populated primarily by Eastern faces, is from a Western man! I begin to wonder what I did to make Mick think I might be interested in him. We were having a good time, laughing, joking, and I did think he was a fun person. Did I project more than I wanted to when my guard was down?

No, no. This is not your fault. Don't fall into that trap.

A friend recently told me that she thought it "unhealthy" for me to insulate myself so much from men. But I know why I do it. It creates a space factor, like a charged electrical field around me, which will shock anyone who ventures too close. I think that invisible barrier, and the attitude it projects, has protected me from other unfortunate incidents with men.

Now I know my awareness must go beyond the stranger on the street, that my guard must be in place at all times. To be left alone at all might mean being completely alone. But I would rather be alone, even lonely, as I have often been, than to compromise myself and feel violated.

In the morning, I board a bus for the ancient city of Pollonaruwa, where colossal stone Buddhas are carved out of a rock wall. One of the imposing figures is standing, and he must be 40 feet high. Beside him, a reclining Buddha is even longer than the other is tall. I cannot help but feel humble in their graceful magnificence.

All over the world I have felt that the art which results from devotion is the most moving of all.

Or is all art a result of some form of devotion?

Several hours later, I climb up a rickety wooden stairway straight up the vertical face of "lion rock" to the sky fortress of Sigiriya. The lion's paws carved into the bottom of the massive outcropping are the source of its nickname. Shaky scaffolding leads under a rock overhang which has protected and preserved some ancient Buddhist frescoes. More steep stairways and a rope ladder lead to the fortress ruins at the top.

The ascent is precarious and I try not to look down. It is a true test of my borderline courage in high places. The reward is a sweeping view and an exhilarating sense of accomplishment.

As the time comes to leave the sky fortress, I realize that going down will be even harder. There is no avoiding looking down. The descent keeps my nerves taut and my eyes on my feet. One missed step on the splintering scaffolding could be disastrous. I make it a walking meditation. Lift foot, move foot, place foot down.

And don't forget to breathe.

I reach the bottom, knees shaking. Looking back up, I am amazed at what I have done. It is even better than learning to ride a bicycle, or driving a car. I feel great. I am ready for anything. *Himalayas, here I come!*

The next day I arrive in the town of Kandy, considered to be the heart of Buddhism in Sri Lanka. The Temple of the Tooth, which supposedly contains a tooth of the Buddha among its relics, rises in pink splendor at the edge of serene Kandy Lake. The evening worship, *puja*, is crowded and noisy, and the driving beat of drums matches the pounding tempo of the pouring rain outside.

I have never witnessed so much activity and commotion at a Buddhist temple before, or so much religious ritual. People pile flowers and food and bright trinkets on offering tables around the temple and in front of the Buddha images, stopping to chant and pray loudly. It is not a particularly peaceful place, and makes me wonder about Buddhism as a religion, which is quite different from the "Art of Living" Goenka-ji teaches at *Dhammagiri*.

How does it all fit together?

I decide to look for some answers, and start by pulling a letter out of the papers in my duffle bag. It is from Nyanaponika Thera, an old German man who has lived as a Buddhist monk in Sri Lanka for many years, studying and writing books about Buddhism.

I had read about him while planning the journey, and wrote a letter asking him if we could meet. He responded warmly, welcoming me, and suggested that I get directions to his Forest Hermitage from the people at the Buddhist Publication Society by the shore of Kandy Lake.

The walk to Nayanaponika's takes me on a lovely path through tall trees rustling with movement and sound. I look up, wondering what kind of birds are being so active and noisy, and am surprised to see hundreds of screeching monkeys hanging from the high branches. I hurry my footsteps along the path, arriving at last at the Forest Hermitage.

The door is opened by a tall pale man of advancing age in the orange robes and shaven head of the Theravadan Buddhist Monk. He greets me with a smile and I present his letter as my introduction.

The small cottage is lined with books and his desk is piled high with papers. He is obviously a very busy man, and I feel that I am intruding. But he offers me a chair and asks what he can do for me.

"I'm having a problem understanding something," I begin. "I learned from my meditation teacher, Sri Goenka, that Buddha never claimed to be a deity, only a man who became enlightened by experiencing the Ultimate Truth for himself, and then taught others a path to liberation from suffering through purification of the mind: seeing and accepting things exactly as they are. If Buddha was not a god and could not answer prayers, why do the people at the Temple of the Tooth perform so much religious ritual? What does one have to do with the other? I am confused."

He smiles at me patiently. "I don't believe that Buddha ever wanted to be worshipped in such a way. He didn't teach 'Buddhism,' he taught *Dhamma* – the truth of the law of nature – which is what your teacher has taught you. But some people will always have to make an 'ism' out of the world's great teachings, and build religions around the teachers.

"Devotional practice is very popular in Asia. Even if some of the people down at the temple were fortunate enough to be exposed to pure *Dhamma* as you have been, the discipline needed to walk the path of self-purification that the Buddha

164

taught is difficult, as you may have discovered. So they simply express their devotion to his qualities of wisdom and compassion through various rites and rituals, instead of actually following the path he taught. But there is no harm done. Whatever they do to pay respect to the qualities of the Buddha will help to bring those positive qualities into their own lives. It is better than nothing."

On the way back to town I think about our talk and my personal feelings about organized religion versus personal spirituality. It seems to me that many followers of religion tend to put the responsibility for their salvation outside themselves, into the hands of God, or Allah, or even Buddha. That just wouldn't work for me. With what I have experienced so far, it has already become clear to me that the responsibility for my salvation – and my happiness – is in my own hands.

I return to the Buddhist Publication Society and pick up a small pamphlet, *Buddhism: A Method of Mind-Training*. It explains that although Buddhism is generally regarded as a religion because it possesses many of the surface characteristics that are associated with religion, it is actually a way of life based on the training of the mind.

"It is not theistic, since it affirms that the universe is governed by impersonal laws and not by any creator-God; it has no use for prayer, for the Buddha was a teacher and not a god; and it regards devotion not as a religious obligation but as a means of expressing gratitude to its founder and as a means of self-development."

A way of life. A way of life that feels right for me.

I am a Jewish Buddhist! (Or would that be a Buddhist Jew?) This is the first path that has ever made any sense to me.

A day of walking around Kandy lake, alone and lonely. A day of reflection and confusion. And such agitation. Should I go here, go there, go today, go tomorrow . . . endless chatter of the mind. How quickly equanimity eludes me.

Walking toward me is an old *sadhu* in a faded orange robe with long white hair and beard, golden skin, broken teeth and sparkling eyes. In passing, we exchange a sympathetic smile which deepens into a look of profound understanding. It is as if we know each other's innermost thoughts; a fleeting instant in which we clearly feel each others' struggle and the struggles of all people. My eyes well with tears.

How easy it is to connect very deeply for a moment, with a stranger.

I'm craving more time in Asia. I want to feel so many places, but I fear I will only be able to see them. Madras, Delhi, the Taj Mahal, the River Ganges, Bodhgaya where the Buddha became enlightened; but then, at last, to Kathmandu and the mountains of Nepal.

Still, as I move quickly around India, maybe bypassing the very essence I seek, I know that I have gained something exceptional. While all the illusions are certainly not gone, I do have a clearer perspective, less clouded by the past, less judgmental, less affected by mental concepts. Some of the garbage has, indeed, been dumped along the way, allowing me a peephole through which I have begun to not only "see things as they really are," but also to feel the truth of who I really am.

It looks like my journal will not be big enough to record all that I could write; nor can I possibly put it all down. My mind's eye will have to be the guardian of the myriad thoughts, memories and dreams that don't choose to form themselves into words.

166

I also realize that so many visual images I cherish most will never be photographed, never be captured by the lens, and I see less and less need to "capture" them at all. Even when the pictures have faded from my conscious mind, their indelible effect will remain printed in my memory, upon the fabric of my being.

Crashing waves. Vermilion sunsets. Old crones at the fish market, sitting on their withered haunches, smoking fat cheroots, haggling over prices and flopping the fresh catch into shoppers' baskets. Toothless smiles, faded *lungis*, chocolate skin, white hair. Do they experience acceptance of their life as it is? Or desperation?

And I, a stranger, wealthy by their standards, from a magical place far away, long to know their simple way of life. What is this human trait of dissatisfaction? If we could trade places, it wouldn't change a thing. The only thing that stays the same is change. *Anicca.*

*For myself, indeed, I now know that
I have traveled so much because travel
has enabled me to arrive at new, unknown
places within my own clouded self.*

Laurens van der Post

Room for One More

Madras may be India's fourth largest city, but it looks and feels more like a sprawling village. There are none of the modern high-rise buildings which punctuate the skyline of Bombay, and bicycles far outnumber motor vehicles on the few paved avenues. The general attitude of the people is also warm and relaxed, in the way that I have found the southern parts of other countries and continents to be.

After the respite of peaceful, Buddhist Sri Lanka, it is exciting to be back in fluorescent, Hindu India. The chaotic vibration is not so foreign now, the kinetic energy not so disturbing.

On Kutchery Street in the southern part of the city, the Kapaleeswarar Temple looms high in the sky above me. Hundreds of carved Hindu gods and goddesses are perched upon its soaring tower, looking poised and ready to leap off and fly away at any moment.

Inside the huge temple, long passageways lead to large open halls. Colorful enameled statues of various Hindu deities

171

are enshrined in alcoves along the walls. Their psychedelic features embody every possible quality – both human and other-worldly.

A four-armed goddess reaches out to me, the third eye in the center of her forehead radiating wisdom and compassion. Nearby, in surprising contrast, a blood red, demonic-looking image assaults me with its bulging eyes, sharp fangs and terrifying expression.

I get the eerie feeling that they act as mirrors; that their purpose is to reflect the myriad hidden parts of myself – to reveal me to myself.

In a dim sanctuary, a priest chants prayers by the flickering light of butter candles and performs rituals with flowers, water and fire. He wears only an orange loincloth wrapped around his hips. His head is shaven, his face and body are decorated with stripes of ash, his bare stomach is large and protruding. The air is hazy with incense. My head begins to swim, and I back out of the small chamber, glad to be in the large open spaces of the temple again.

Men and woman prostrate themselves in devotion to their deities everywhere within the enormous structure, but I am mystified by the actions of one wrinkled old woman. She kneels, touches her head to the ground three times, then stands up, crosses her arms in front of her breasts and pulls on opposite ear lobes three times while bouncing up and down, then pounds her fists into her temples three times.

What does it all mean?

I ask a *Sikh* who is also watching the old woman's ritual. He thinks for a moment, stroking his black beard, then asks me a question in reply.

172

"You sing songs, called hymns, in the churches of your country, do you not?"

"Yes," I nod.

"And the purpose of the hymn is to praise God?"

I nod again.

"Then you see, what she is doing is like a hymn — in motion."

Ah, India. Where the bizarre and the beautiful are one.

I hire a bicycle *ricksha* to take me to the tourist office. The driver has graying hair and betel-red teeth. The sinewy muscles in his aging legs work feverishly as he pedals the long, uphill grade. He is so delighted when I tip him an extra *rupee*, little more than a dime, that he fairly beams as he salutes me. Perhaps that one *rupee* means his family will have more than just rice and *chapatis* to eat tonight.

The tourist office is closed for lunch, so I go to the rickety stall at the corner where a few local men are drinking *chai*. The proprietor rummages around beneath his counter, and then, with a grand flourish, presents my tea in a cracked white cup and saucer instead of the ordinary glass. I exaggerate a bow in return, and we have a good laugh. As the other customers laugh along with us, something clicks inside me.

It is like the final piece of a jigsaw puzzle clicking into place. A moment of clarity which ties the whole picture together. A moment of great satisfaction. A moment of understanding that *I fit in*. No longer just observing from the outside, but existing as an integral part of the scene.

It has taken two months, and I'm finally comfortable here.

More than comfortable.

Joyful.

I have never felt this way when traveling before, and I have traveled a lot. But on this solo journey of mine there is no cushion, no place to hide. No companion to take refuge in; no protective barrier to keep me from reaching out or discourage others from reaching in. Being on my own has forced me to take risks, to be vulnerable, to call upon my own resources, to remember the truth of who I am. To be that truth.

And I am convinced that one big reason I have come to the place of joy within myself in this strangest of all environments, is because I am here *alone*.

I get the directions I need from the Tourist Office, and walk several blocks to a bus stop. Along comes the dilapidated bus to Tiruvannamalai, bursting at the rusted seams.

I push my way through the door over the protestations of the conductor.

"No room! Next bus!" he shouts at me, but I have learned that the next will be no better.

There's always room for one more.

Squeezing my way through the congested coach, I wiggle into an empty spot on the crowded aisle floor. My seat is my duffel bag and my view the splayed toes and cracked heels of generations of barefoot lives, packed tightly together.

But I am on the bus. One more small challenge. One more great victory.

Soon, we are out of the city and heading south. I'm glad I cannot see out the window, because the incessant shrill horn honking and the intermittent gasps and cheers of the passengers tells me there is a race going on. As we lunge back and forth across the road, playing chicken with oncoming traffic, I wonder how my family would ever find out if I died in an obscure bus accident somewhere in the bowels of India.

"You are traveling alone, Madam?" I look up to see a bearded man in a bright blue turban peering at me intently. A dark eyed woman with an ornately jeweled ring in her nose peeks over his shoulder.

"You know, that is quite unusual in our country," he says.

Before I can reply, a loud clunk brings us to a lurching halt, dumping me the short distance to the floorboards. It sounds suspiciously like the motor has fallen out.

Gingerly unfolding myself from the tangle of grumbling passengers, bleating goats and scattered baskets of vegetables, I inch my way back and out through the door of the disabled vehicle into a blast of mid-day heat.

Shielding my eyes, I see the turbaned man open a large umbrella. He kindly motions for me to join his wife under the big black canopy for protection from the burning sun. She smiles shyly behind the veil of her sari and offers me an orange in her outstretched hand.

As I bite into the refreshing fruit, I am touched by their concern for me, a stranger alone in their country. How grateful I am to be traveling in a way that offers me the greatest opportunity to intimately experience the place I am visiting, the people who live here, and, most importantly, the many parts of myself.

The trying times are more than balanced by the moments of delight, and insight, I experience while traveling on my own.

In ten minutes we are back on the road. The fix seems too quick to me. I steel myself for another jolt to the floor, but am pleasantly surprised. The next thirty minutes pass uneventfully, and we pull into a roadside tea stall for a rest stop.

Twenty-five *paise*, the equivalent of three cents, buys me a glass of South Indian milk-coffee. The glass is taken from a murky water bucket, rinsed with two swipes of the hand, and filled from a large tin pot kept warm over small coals. I briefly consider the water bucket, and more carefully consider the hand, but ultimately realize that the only way to have anything here is to take it exactly the way it comes. I think the people of India learned that lesson long ago.

I stop in at the ladies "toilet" – a nearby wall out in the open – and wade through the puddles to an empty spot. It looks like it has been hosed down pretty recently. A pleasant change.

As the journey resumes, and all the passengers return to their rightful places on the crowded bus, I move to one side of my "seat" and offer an old woman the other half of the duffel bag. She smiles at me in grateful thanks, her few teeth stained blood red from years of chewing betel-nut, and plants herself, blessing me. Shriveled chocolate breasts peek out from behind her white widow's sari. Her ear lobes hang long, the now-empty holes enlarged from the size and weight of her earrings over the years. There are more holes filled with little rings all the way around her ear and three jewels in her nose as well. She is trying to communicate something to me, but we cannot get any kind of a verbal open line. I just keep smiling and nodding; it makes us both feel good.

The horn continues to honk, the bus continues to sway, and I continue to be amazed that I am here, wondering at the motivation which drives me forward and where it's taking me.

Each time I find myself like this, on the floor of an Indian bus crunched within a mass of humanity, or some similar outrageous situation by the standards of my "previous" life, I can't believe it's me doing it.

Well, it is me. And I am doing it. Believe it.

I don't relate to the word "brave," which people continue to use to describe me with respect to this journey. To my mind, brave is the attitude of a warrior, a hero. Me? I'm just following an internal compass that guides me. Staying on course. Moving through fear, and crowded buses.

Head cradled in folded arms, a flash flood of emotion suddenly rises up through my chest and spills out my eyes, allowing a clearer view of my inner resources and personal motivation to come into focus.

A warrior? No way. A hero? Not hardly. "Brave?"

I'll take it.

But if you travel far enough, one day you will recognize yourself coming down the road to meet yourself. And you will say YES.

Marion Woodman

Fools Rush In

I arrive in Tiruvannamalai as darkness begins to fall.

Thank goodness I didn't wait for the "next bus."

A smiling barefoot boy with a bicycle *ricksha* appears. "*Ashram, Memsahib*?" He correctly assumes that westerners only come to this out-of-the-way town to visit the *ashram* of the well-known, now deceased guru Ramana Maharshi.

I nod my assent. My "unplanned" journey has become more of a pilgrimage along the way, and I am marking the map to visit spiritual places and teachers to which I am drawn. I had read about Ramana Maharshi's *ashram* and decided that it would be worth a short side trip to visit the center of this enlightened master.

The *ricksha* driver tells me it will be eight *rupees*. His smile is charming and disarming. I say okay, and off we go. His young legs are already as fibrous as the legs of an old man from the strain of peddling people and baggage around town; but he sings in a high voice all the way to the *ashram*.

During the ride I notice that there are very few motorized vehicles in the town, and no other westerners in sight. I am completely off the beaten track, and I feel excited, almost high. It is not long before I remember that whenever the pendulum swings too far in one direction, *Anicca* is not far behind. My pride soon turns to embarrassment.

At the *ashram*, the *ricksha walla* takes the eight *rupees* I hand him and touches it to his forehead. He pedals away, singing at the top of his lungs again. No wonder he is so happy. An Indian man watching from the porch tells me I have paid about double the normal fare for the ride.

"Never be taking the first price you are given, Madam," he admonishes me. "Always strike a deal. Prices are very flexible here in India."

My face turns red. Of course I know better. I should have bargained, but his smile was just so charming . . .

Why do I feel like such a chump? That ricksha driver needs the extra few cents a lot worse than I do.

I enter the office and request accommodation for the night.

"Have you written to us for a room, Madam?" the male clerk asks.

"No, I just thought . . .".

"You just thought you could come on your whim and be given lodging here at the *ashram*?"

My face turns red for the second time in five minutes. I feel like a kid who had her hand slapped, and deserved it.

How presumptuous of me to assume I could walk blithely in here and be welcomed with open arms. How ignorant I am to think there will be a place for me wherever and whenever I decide to show up.

Many other western visitors must have come with the same self-centered assumptions, based on the attitude of the clerk. But after rummaging around for a few minutes, he comes up with "the last available room" and hands me a key. Clean and bright, it turns out to be one of the nicest rooms I've had in all of India.

The main hall of the *ashram* is dominated by an enormous black and white photo of Ramana Maharshi on the wall. His face has the quality of an innocent child. His eyes are wells of compassion. Although he has been dead since the early 1950's, people still come to study his teachings and worship whatever lingers of his mystical presence. Two old devotees in matching white beards and white dhotis bend their bowed legs with difficulty to prostrate themselves before the guru's shrine.

This feels like religion again. Worship. Looking outside oneself for salvation, instead of exploring within. Do they think he's a guru, or a god? I don't know. Maybe it's really all the same.

Two western women in Indian dress walk by and ignore me. I feel less and less comfortable in this "spiritual" center.

The beggars that wait outside the *ashram* wail at me. "Maaa, Maaa" they cry, hauntingly. I don't know if there is a particular meaning to what they say or if it is just a plaintive lament. To their chagrin, I resist giving handouts much more easily these days, though they are definitely persistent. One snowy bearded old man actually raises his walking stick in anger at me for not sharing my wealth with him.

At dinner hour all the pilgrims sit cross legged on the stone floor of the dining hall. A placemat of leaves sewn by hand is put before each of us. One server comes along with a bucket and puts a scoop of rice on my mat. Another comes by and pours *dal* over the rice. A third hands out *chapatis*. I am hungry, and though the fare is plain I devour every bit of food, scraping the mat clean with my fingers. At the end of the meal, I am sad to see the lovely hand-sewn leaf plates thrown away.

As in most spiritual communities in India, there is no fee charged to pilgrims for either room or board. Donations are purely voluntary, to be placed in marked boxes.

After dinner the same office clerk approaches me.

"You have traveled from America, Madam, a very rich country, and we have arranged accommodation for you in our crowded center without a prior notice from you. Everything here is given free of charge, but other people from your country and from European countries have come and given us nothing at all."

Ah. So not only do we westerners show up expecting to be welcomed, we leave without putting any rupees in the box.

"Here is an envelope for your donation, Madam. Please return it to me." At that, he turns and walks away.

I look at the envelope and feel irritated. What happened to donations being "voluntary?" Am I to be responsible for all those who have come before me?

I am happy to contribute. I am not happy to be pressured. I look forward to leaving the next day.

On my morning walk I become part of the stream of motion in the awakening streets. Bright *saris* paint the new day with color as women carry polished brass jugs on their heads to the local water spout to fill their vessels and share gossip; kiosks are set up for a business and dirt walkways are religiously swept; children collect cow dung along the road and form it into patties to dry for fuel; bicycles swish past holy cows and bullock carts, ringing their warning bells.

And I, like some transparent bird, float through it all softly, as in a dream. Existing, yet not really being a part of this world; touching for a moment, yet leaving no mark upon the lives of these people. It is as if I am invisible to them. Only the peacock across the way screams at me in recognition.

The *ricksha* driver waiting outside the *ashram* at noon agrees to a fare of five *rupees* for the ride back to the bus station. He tells me where to wait for the bus back to Madras.

While I am waiting, a young fellow calling himself a "bus agent" comes to inform me that the bus to Madras will not stop where I am standing. He picks up my bag and carries it for me across the street. "This is the correct waiting place, Madam," he says, holding out his hand for *baksheesh*. After I give him some coins, he disappears. And so does the bus to Madras. From across the street. Without me.

For the third time in two days I feel foolish. This time I have been taken by a con man, pretending to help me. Have these street-wise kids no other choice but to cheat unsuspecting visitors to make a few *rupees*? Even as I ask myself the question, I know the answer. In a country as overcrowded as India, there are few choices available.

Reaching Madras at last as the dark closes in, I take a "seven *rupee* special" shared accommodation at the Broadlands Lodge.

Entering the small room quietly, I try not to disturb the lady already asleep in the other bed. I can hear the neighbors on both sides talking through the flimsy partitions which divide the cubicles.

Soon an irritated Australian man yells to his roommate,

"Turn out the light already, will ya mate!"

My roommate stirs and quotes softly in a youthful British voice, " 'Poor are those who have no patience.' I think India must be very rich."

Sadhu. Sadhu. Sadhu. Well said, my friend, well said.

Though we travel the world over to find the beautiful, we must carry it with us, or we find it not.

Ralph Waldo Emerson

Happy Birthday Rama

Twenty-two sweltering hours on the train from Madras to Bombay is a grueling experience. I get little sleep on the plank they call a "berth" in second class and arrive bone weary and dehydrated.

It is 9:00 p.m. and dark. The March air is heavy with humidity. I decide it is too late to walk in on the Jahandra family, and begin the search for a cheap hotel room that takes me from one teeming street to another.

At night, Bombay feels like a city that ate too much. Its clogged intestines are bloated with humanity. Belching and passing gas to relieve the pressure, it leaves a noxious stench and a thick, greasy film where the air should be. Worst of all, its putrid excrement fills every gutter with the homeless, the hungry, the diseased and the dying.

I become completely exhausted by the futile search for lodging. Each time I ask to use a telephone, the answer is "telephone not working." Along the roads, the hustlers and the beggars, the smoke and the noise, the traffic and the crush of bodies grate harshly at my ragged edges.

189

A sharp-eyed boy of about twelve hones in when he sees me dejectedly leaving two neighboring hotels. His smile is disarming. He knows of a place "just up the street." I look at him for a long time. He pouts. "Don't you trust me, miss lady?"

Do I dare?

He earns his *baksheesh*. The shabby room with peeling redflecked wallpaper and resident cockroach family feels like the perfect ending for my stay in Bombay. At least it affords me some privacy, something I would never get at Rina's.

I have heard other people describe their "love/hate" feelings for India. In my sleazy hotel room at 11:00 p.m. in the still vibrating city, the hate feelings become predominant for me. I feel way off balance. Completely out of whack.

Maybe it's because I'm stressed out from traveling such long distances. Maybe it's because I haven't been doing any meditation lately. Maybe it's because I haven't had a menstrual period for the last two months. I wonder why?

After a quick stop by the Jahandra's to pick up my hiking boots, I head to the rail ticket reservation office. When I am told there is simply no space available on the afternoon train to Delhi, I start to cry. "But I cannot stay in Bombay!" I sob. My tears go on until the poor clerk wrings his hands and says he will do his best to get me on the train, and come back at noon.

I go back to my room to wait. I berate myself for having gone from feeling so strong to being totally drained and reactive. I wonder if I've gained anything at all from India, except adeptness at pushing myself onto crowded buses. Worries about what to do when I return home haunt me, and I question again how the journey will benefit me in the long run.

190

Fool! How could it not? An invisible, indelible impression. A growth immeasurable. Changed? Yes. No. I don't know.

All that matters is that you are aware. And equanimous. Could you just remember to watch your sensations for a change?

Oh. Sensations. I forgot.

Obviously.

Like a salve being spread on an open wound, taking the time to observe the reality within myself takes the sting away. As I continue to sit and pay attention to the change taking place throughout my body, the awareness of impermanence, *anicca,* calms my mind and begins the healing process.

At noon I return to the ticket office, prepared to accept the reality exactly as it is. I know I can handle whatever I have to do next. It's all so temporary, so momentary. Bombay. The journey. My life.

The clerk hands me a first-class ticket to Delhi.

"That will be three hundred and thirty *rupees,* Madam. The train departs Bombay Central at 5:00 p.m."

Although thirty-three dollars for a first-class ticket puts a good dent in my second-class budget, I am grateful to be on the train at all. Sharing the compartment with me are Mary from San Francisco, also traveling solo, and two Indian men.

Mary tells me that she is doing her graduate studies in Hindi language and that she has traveled extensively in India. The clean-shaven man says he is traveling on business. The other man wears the close dark beard and elaborate turban of the Sikh religion, and says nothing about himself.

As the journey progresses, the men begin to ask Mary and me questions about our lives and our country. We find explaining the attitudes of liberal American women to them an exasperating task. Try as they might, and as "modern" as they think they are, the cultural gulf is simply too wide.

It is a complete mystery to them why we would choose to travel alone, why we are not married, and why we do not have any children. Mary and I just look at each other and roll our eyes. As valuable as it's been to travel alone, it is fun to have a female companion for a change.

Mary and I decide to share a room in Delhi. It is comforting to have the support of someone who knows where she is going in the city after dark. We check in at the New Delhi YMCA. Our room is spotless, and I am delighted to have her as a roommate.

The next day, Mary heads out to find some Hindi books. I decide to take a city bus tour to get an overall look at Delhi, and am pleasantly surprised. New Delhi is like a different world away from Bombay. Clean, broad, tree-lined avenues, and very few families living on the streets. There is space to move, room to breathe.

The bus drives past embassies and consulates and big estates set back behind wrought iron gates. We visit the Nehru Memorial and Raj Ghat, the monument marking the site of Mahatma Gandhi's cremation.

Each time we return to the bus we are approached by souvenir vendors and snake charmers. Even the hawkers become silent when the strains of the bamboo flute entice the cobra to rise out of his basket and flare his hood menacingly while he sways back and forth to the music.

The coach then heads for "Old" Delhi, a maze of narrow alleyways and ancient mildewed buildings. It stops at the seventeenth century Red Fort, with its graceful archways and tall red brick towers. While the other tourists explore the inside of the historic fort, I discover the crowded, colorful bazaar brimming with activity just outside the huge gates.

We are also taken to Jama Masjid, the largest mosque in India. It is the first time I have been in an Islamic place of worship, and I am surprised to discover that it has the most "spiritual" feeling of all the religious places I've visited. There are no priests, no images, no ceremony. Just the wailing call to prayer from the towering minarets and the courtyard filled with hundreds of people kneeling and bowing toward Mecca.

My feelings about India are coming into balance again.
Love, hate, love, hate, anicca, anicca, anicca.

After the tour, I decide to telephone Kuldeep Mohan. His name had been given to me as a contact in Delhi by my friend Arlene in California.

Happily, he sounds delighted to hear from me. He remembers our mutual friend fondly, and immediately invites me to his home for lunch the next day.

The following noon I hail a "three-wheeler," a motorized *ricksha* also called a scooter or a "tuk tuk" because the motor sounds like tuk tuk tuk tuk tuk. It takes me on a hair-raising ride to an upper class house on the outskirts of the city.

Kuldeep greets me at the door. He seems a kind and gentle man in his early forties. As he shows me around his lovely home, complete with western style toilets and toilet paper, he tells me that he works out of his home in the carpet exporting business, and that he travels to Britain and other parts of Europe for his work.

He also explains that he is divorced and has custody of his two sons, which he says he knows is generally different from America but is typical in India. This is because the father usually has a higher income to take care of the children. It sounds like they don't have child support battles in India.

Kuldeep apparently has many western friends and entertains foreign visitors in his home quite often.

"The list keeps growing as people continue to give each other my name!"

It is easy to see why. He is a gracious host. Many of us have come through the meditation "grapevine," as Kuldeep has also studied *Vipassana* with Goenka.

Kuldeep's "kitchen boy" serves us a marvelous meal of spicy chicken *vindaloo* in a vinegar marinade, curried mixed vegetables, rice with nuts and raisins, and *raita*, yogurt blended with cucumber and spices. Kuldeep eats with a combination of fork and fingers. I follow his lead, using freshly baked *paratha* to scoop up vegetables and rice and chicken until my plate is perfectly clean.

Over lunch he asks about my friend in America, *(She's very well)*; if I found the meditation course to be difficult, *(That's putting it mildly);* whether I do yoga, *(I'd love to find a teacher here)*; and my impressions of India, *(Do you have a week?)*.

When I express my admiration for the relatively uninhabited streets of Delhi, he explains that the homeless and beggars are being rounded up and put in shelters to clean up the city for the upcoming Asian Games, a regional version of the Olympics. He comments that it is more pleasant for him, too. His clipped English accent and attitude of *savoir-faire* give the impression that he is as much "western" as he is Indian.

Kuldeep generously invites me to be a guest in his home, but I explain that I am moving quickly along to see a few more places in India before making my way to Kathmandu, Nepal.

My spring trek in the Himalayas will begin in two weeks, and getting from place to place in India has taken more time than I thought it would.

Have I already been here two months?

He urges me to come back after Nepal and stay, to which I happily agree.

In the morning I tell Mary that I am going to the post office to see if I have any mail and to the train station to buy tickets.

"No you're not," she says.

"I'm not?"

"Everything is closed today. It's an Indian holiday. Rama's Birthday. He's the hero of the Ramayana, one of the most important historical legends of India. We're going to a parade."

Chadni Chowk, the silver market street in the center of Old Delhi, is jammed. People are hanging out of upper story windows, yelling and waving. Musicians in gold lame' costumes blow horns and bang drums, competing with the ever-present high-pitched recorded music blaring from loudspeakers. Food of every kind is distributed for the taking, most of which is taken by holy cows meandering through the excited crowd.

What a spectacle it is, and what chaos.

Makeshift "floats" move through the center of the crowd, carrying people costumed and made up as the characters from the epic story.

The god Krishna, renowned for his exploits with the young milkmaids called *gopis*, is portrayed by a handsome adolescent boy enshrined on the back of a rusted flat-bed truck. Garlands of orange flowers hang around his neck and his smooth skin is dyed a rich blue. Cascading black curls, long dark lashes and crimson lips complete the innocent, yet sensual, picture.

As the mood and tempo of the celebration grow in intensity, my body begins to vibrate in the hot, moist afternoon. The rhythmic pulsing in the streets courses through me like a million fingertips, stimulating every pore, every erogenous zone.

A combination of my greatest dreams and my worst nightmares, India is a psychedelic kaleidoscope of color, movement, sound and smell – a kaleidoscope that threatens to sweep me into its frenetic pattern and take me to that edge where control begins to lose its grip on abandon.

It would be easy to lose myself in India.

That's the place to get to — nowhere.
One wants to wander away from the
world's somewheres, into our own nowhere.

D.H. Lawrence

To Be Loved

The "Pink City Express" transports me from Delhi to the state of Rajasthan, known as the legendary land of chivalry. The "Abode of Kings."

The rail line ends in Jaipur, where I find a small city built entirely of soft pink sandstone whose hues dissolve from orchid to peach to rose to amber to magenta in the changing light of day. The women wear short blouses and wide colorful skirts decorated with tiny round mirrors. Chunky silver jewelry hangs from their necks, arms, ankles, noses. Even their toes wear silver rings. Tall, ruggedly handsome men sport huge handlebar mustaches and bright turbans. It is vibrant and I am excited. Being in Rajasthan feels like being in another India.

Standing on the main street in the center of downtown, I look up at *Hawa Mahal*, the Palace of the Winds. A towering facade of rosy sandstone, it allowed the Maharaja's cloistered ladies to look out at parades and festivals without being seen. I can almost imagine veiled ladies peeping through the intricate cut-outs, wishing they could disguise themselves as birds and fly down to alight on the back of a prancing horse.

Seven miles out of Jaipur, I climb into the *howdah* on the back of a gaily dressed elephant for a trip up the steep hill to Amber Fort, the abandoned fortress-palace of the Maharajah. Giving him an apple, the *mahout* speaks softly to the elephant, patting him gently as we go. The beast is so big and heavy that as it lumbers up the hill I am gently rocked from side to side, soothed almost to sleep by the swaying motion.

Later, resting at a tea stall, I watch a family of pigs grovel around in the deep gutters of Jaipur, acting as a clean-up crew by eating the waste products of human beings. It reminds me of the last time I saw the snorting creatures at work, in Kingston, Jamaica, a dozen years ago on my first trip outside the USA. I remember being repulsed, not only by the pigs burying their snouts in the muck, but by the poverty and filth in general. It was painful to see malnourished children peeping out of shacks made of tar paper and tin. Only twenty years old myself at the time, I was shocked and humiliated that human beings actually lived like that. How little I had been exposed to the realities beyond my own protected world. I could only avert my eyes, hoping it would all go away.

I no longer avert my eyes at the suffering of others, but accept that this, too, is part of the reality of life as it is. I can watch it change, but I cannot change it. I can only honor every being for doing the best they can with the situation in which they find themselves. India is teaching me something about survival, humility and compassion.

At dinner in the Jaipur Government Circuit House, I converse with two fellows from America who are fascinated to discover that I am traveling alone. The "B" word comes up again: "brave."

It may be true that I don't fear the kind of things that keep most people from traveling alone, but I am afraid of different things which may not seem frightening to others. Wouldn't they all be surprised at the truth! How very easy this seems to me compared to being at home and going on with my life. No wonder I want to stay on and on. It's an easy out. The ultimate procrastination.

The real test of bravery for me will be when I feel good about going home, and make courageous decisions when I get there. I want to stop running from, and start running to something in my life.

The city of Agra, host to that wonder of the world the Taj Mahal, has more flies than I have ever seen in one place in my life. As I walk through the open market on my first afternoon, they buzz around my face, dive-bombing my eyes. I stop short at the stall of a dry goods seller, not believing what I see. Large open trays are piled high with bulk flour, rice and lentils for sale. The surface of the food is covered with hundreds of crawling flies.

I feel sick to my stomach, and hail a *ricksha* to take me to the Taj Mahal.

A little ways down the road, a mop-haired teenage boy on a rusted bicycle rides up close to the *ricksha*, reaches over and touches my arm, and says what may be the only English words he knows: "fucky, fucky?" I shoo him away, like a huge annoying fly, but he sticks close and touches me again. Finally I give him a shove that sends him and his bicycle reeling. He looks genuinely surprised, and I wonder what he really expected?

The *ricksha* driver turns off the main road to the Taj Mahal and takes me on a side trip to a nearby marble factory where he tries to convince me to make a purchase (on which he would make a commission, of course).

"Look at this beautiful inlaid table. How about a lovely cigarette box, Madam? Some coasters? Only forty *rupees*."

A fly alights on my cheek. A fuse blows in my head.

"If you think being a *ricksha* driver is hard work, you should try being a tourist. I've been nagged, hassled and hustled up to here!" My hand touches my neck.

I get back into the *ricksha*. "Now please let's go. And no more side trips!" He sheepishly gets onto the driver's seat and peddles out into the street.

Thankfully, the Taj Mahal, a monument to an Emperor's love for his deceased wife, makes up for the rest of the town. At first glance it appears to be surreal, as if superimposed upon a painted backdrop of bright blue sky. An exquisite and perfectly balanced structure, the white marble almost quivers with aliveness. It is both delicate and powerful, conjuring a vision out of a fairytale.

Or did the fairytale image in my mind come from seeing pictures of this?

Throngs of Indian tourists swarm like bees around the hive-shaped dome and children run through the formal gardens. The hot afternoon sun, the crowd and the noise are too much for me. I decide to return at sunrise and be the first one through the gate.

The quiet movement in the morning streets does not assault my grateful senses. It is too early for music, for touts, for

202

beggars, for flies. The cycle *ricksha* rolls softly to a stop in front of the imposing red sandstone archway. I pay the driver. He salutes me and rolls away again into the dawn mist.

I hand the ticket seller my two *rupees*, and walk through the arch with bated breath.

I am alone with the Taj Mahal.

Beyond the gardens, the lawns, the trees, it shimmers in the rising light of the sun, mirrored in a long rectangular pool. Is it my imagination, or is the chill air being warmed by an aura of love and beauty which emanates from the pearlescent stone?

Moving slowly, I look from every angle, following the curve of the dome with my eyes, raising them to include the tops of the tapering minarets. Coming closer, my hands caress the smooth inlaid marble surface and feel the empty places where precious inlaid stones have fallen or been taken out.

Leaving my shoes by the door, I walk barefoot inside. The polished tiles are cool on my feet. The air is still. The graceful dome reaches high above me. I stand by the tomb where the Emperor Shah Jahan and his beloved wife, Mumtaz Mahal, are entombed side by side.

It feels like a holy place to me. The holiness of beauty. The sacredness of love.

I speak a word to hear if it will echo. The sound comes back to me. I sing a few notes and am surrounded by the reverberations of my own voice. Then I hear other voices. People are coming. My time alone with the Taj Mahal is over.

I walk back beyond the reflective pool and sit on a stone bench, gazing at the legend, the wonder. I contemplate the fact that in the 1600's it took twenty years and twenty thousand workers to complete. All for love.

The marble glows pink in the dawn light, slowly becoming golden and then pure white as the sun rises higher in the sky, revealing the impermanent and changing nature of the morning, the marble, and my mind.

In the afternoon I take a bus from Agra about twenty miles to Fatepur Sikri, a perfectly preserved red sandstone Mogul fortress city built in the sixteenth century. It is high on my guidebook's list of must-sees. I am left off near the entrance to the abandoned fortress, but am immediately seduced by the village bazaar bursting with life outside its imposing walls. I waver for a moment. Fortress, bazaar. Fortress, bazaar. The bazaar wins.

As I wander down a narrow street lined with tiny open stalls spilling over with fabrics, jewelry, cooking utensils and food, I hear giggling behind me. I turn to see three brightly clad ladies in the bangle seller's shop looking at me and covering their mouths to hide their laughter.

One of them points to my dusty neon-yellow running shoes, and a pretty silly sight they are in a country of flimsy sandals and bare feet. In a flash of inspiration, I pull off my shoes and hand them to her. In delight, she puts them on and dances around, her sari billowing around her. Taking off her new colorful plastic bracelets, she hands them to me, speaking rapidly in Hindi. It is apparent that she wants to make a trade.

Through expressions and gestures, and a little help from the English-speaking proprietor of the shop, I explain that I need to keep my shoes. She sticks out her lower lip in an exaggerated pout, hands me my shoes and takes back her bangles.

Then playfully shaking her head and smiling at me, she puts one of the bright bracelets back on my wrist and pats it, indicating it is mine to keep.

I take her hands in mine, and smiling into each other's eyes, we share a moment that crosses all boundaries of language or culture. We are people. We are women. We are having fun together. We appreciate each other. We honor each other. Bowing slightly, palms together near my heart in the gesture of *Namaste*, I salute her and continue on my way.

Off the beaten track, I am once again the only "foreigner" around, and again I find it strangely stimulating to be in that position. Anonymous. Responsible to no one but myself. Taking each moment as it comes. Creating my journey as I go.

Later at the Agra station, waiting to depart for Delhi, I meet a very tall, good looking, American expatriate. Dirk tells me that he is on vacation from his job in Saudi Arabia. We talk about travel, about philosophy, about life. His blue eyes crinkle almost closed when he laughs, and dimples punctuate his boyish face. When the time comes to board the train, we wave good-bye. He proceeds to the first class car and I sit down in second class.

Shortly after we pull out of the station, the conductor comes to my seat. "Please be coming with me Madam."

"But where are we going?" I ask.

"Not to worry, Madam." I catch a flash of a conspiratorial smile on his lips. "Please be following me."

As I walk behind him, puzzled, he escorts me through several railcars up to the first class compartment and to Dirk, who has paid the difference in price for my ticket so that we can continue our conversation! I am flustered, and flattered. It is the nicest thing anyone has done for me in a long time.

"I really just wanted to see your smile again," he confides a short time later. "There is something about the way you smile that lights up everything around you."

I smile until my cheeks ache, all the way to Delhi.

When we get there, he asks if I will join him for lunch the next day.

I thought you'd never ask.

"Thanks. I'd love to."

At night, in my bed at the YMCA, thoughts and fantasies invade the night, and sleep evades me. I can't stop thinking about him.

I can hardly remember the last time I was so attracted to a man or one responded so strongly to me. I try to keep my romantic illusions at bay, but it's been a long time since I've experienced infatuation, and it's fun. Besides, I really need this kind of attention. I want to wallow in it.

I want to feel loved.

We meet at noon at his hotel and settle down on a cushy sofa in a quiet corner of the lobby. He's made reservations for lunch at a nearby Chinese restaurant in an hour. We talk. And talk. And talk. We share ideas, ponder cosmic questions, tell stories, act silly. He is a warm and intelligent person. I feel totally accepted and valued for exactly who I am. A rare and precious experience.

Then, as if it is the most natural thing in the world, he takes my chin in his hand, pulls my face toward him, and kisses me.

His lips touch mine with such tenderness that I want to cry, but when I suddenly feel the heat rising in my body I pull back and cover my blushing face with my hands. I peek out to see him smiling, and I can't help but smile back. Then he stands up, grabs my hand and announces "lunch time!"

We romantically feed each other Chinese food with chopsticks, open our hearts and spill out our dreams, walk hand-in-hand in the sultry afternoon, share an ice cream cone, retrieve my luggage from the YMCA, hail a taxi for me to catch my train to Varanasi . . . and then a sudden awkwardness descends like a guillotine, cutting the tie that bound us so quickly, so closely. What happens now?

The sadness at parting comes unexpectedly for me, and he can barely look me in the eye to say goodbye. The driver is waiting. I grope for words, say inane things, ask if we can "keep in touch." At that, a shadow of guilt crosses his face and he looks away, pulls away emotionally as surely as if he has turned his back on me.

I get into the cab, feeling vulnerable and exposed and hurt, like eyes that have been in a dark room, suddenly coming out into the brightness of morning. I had wanted to be loved. I got my wish, for a day. But, as Goenka says, "how long happy?"

And what more would I have wanted from it anyway?

On the ride to the station I become aware of the barriers reforming around me, but I have no regrets. The time spent with Dirk makes me realize how much I value quality companionship, and reminds me that I am worthy of being appreciated, admired and loved. In that way, my short time with him was a wonderful gift.

I understand why it has been important for me to be alone. Now I think I'm ready for it to end.

Our battered suitcases were piled on the sidewalk again; we had longer ways to go. But no matter, the road is life.

Jack Kerouac

Life As Drama

No matter how often I feel that India cannot surprise me any more, I continue to be amazed. It is as if every person here is a character, playing a role on the stage of the theatre of life and death.

The ancient city of Benares, renamed Varanasi after India gained independence, is the religious capital of the Hindu faith. It sits alongside the River Ganges, which is the holiest spot in the world to Hindus. It is said that each drop of *Ganga Ma*, Mother River, is sacred, for its waters are believed to hold the power of salvation.

I had read that pilgrims, inspired by their faith in life after death, come to have a dip in the sacred river to wash away their sins, and also take some holy water home with them. Some spend years of their lives traveling hundreds of miles on foot to reach Benares. Many stay to die so that they may be cremated beside the Mother River. That assures a heavenly future.

Drifting in a tour boat in the middle of the river in the misty light of dawn, I am captivated by a time-stopping show.

As the sun rises, it looks as if a million spots of color are seeping out of the narrow alleyways of the ancient city and flowing helter-skelter down the steps leading to the river; and as the boat floats nearer to the shore I see that the colors are actually men, women and children, young and old, healthy and sick, stepping down the *ghat*s to immerse themselves in the holy stream.

People do every imaginable thing at the edge of the Ganges: wash their bodies, scrub their clothes, brush their teeth, clean out their noses, do yoga postures, say prayers, perform rituals, cremate the dead and throw their remains into the river, and who knows what else? The carcass of a cow floats by and raw sewage streams from a pipe into the water. I find it hard to believe in the "Miracle of the Ganges," which says that the flowing water tests bacterially "pure;" but it is certainly miraculous to me that I am here to observe it at all.

During the day I weave my way through the gridlock of pilgrims, cycle *rickshas* and holy cows which jam the narrow pathways of Benares, stepping over piles of cow dung and sewage-filled gutters. It is my goal to visit a few of the multitude of temples which are tucked in between the countless rows of tiny stalls selling religious objects and beautiful silk brocades.

My first stop is the Golden Temple of Viswanatha, which is dedicated to Lord *Shiva*, both the "Destroyer" and the "Reproducer" in the Hindu cosmology. I guess this temple is devoted to the "reproduction" part. The focus of worship is a giant-sized phallic symbol called a *lingam*. Water drips down the *lingam* into a vulva-like receptacle called a *yoni*. Oil candles flicker everywhere in the dim light. The sexual energy is palpable, undulating in waves throughout the temple and around my body. It feels dark and invasive to me, and I want to shake it off.

Some devotees of *Shiva*, holy men who have renounced worldly life, sit outside the temple, naked bodies streaked with ash, hair a mass of tangled dreadlocks. They are bleary-eyed from too much meditation, or more likely too much hashish.

Next I go to the temple of *Durga,* the Goddess of Power, where there is a powerful statue of the half-man-half-monkey-god *Hanuman*, who is worshipped as a symbol of physical strength, perseverance and devotion. Real monkeys, wiry and aggressive, cavort everywhere and even reach into my pockets looking for food.

At other shrines I meet the god *Ganesha* again, the boy with the head of an elephant, and *Kali*, The Goddess of Fire, who has eight arms, wears a necklace of skulls and breathes the flame of destruction.

By the end of the afternoon I come away from these varied Hindu places of worship with a head full of discordant images and a feeling of prickling agitation.

Where can I find some peace?

I decide to go to the nearby Deer Park of Sarnath, where Buddha preached his first sermon after becoming enlightened. The moment the bus leaves the outskirts of the city and the countryside comes into view, I am able to breathe easier.

The outsides of the houses along the way appear to be decorated with various patterns of large brown circles. At a turn in the road I see a woman pulling the circles off the wall of her home and stacking them into a pile in her front yard. It is then that I realize that the "decorations" are actually cow dung patties which have been stuck on the walls and left to dry, to be recycled as fuel for cooking and heating.

How ingenious. The things we do to survive.

The bus leaves me at the edge of a large green park. In the middle of the grass is a tall circular sandstone *stupa*, a Buddhist shrine. There are a few trees, rustling in the warm wind. There are no other people. It is quiet.

I sit on the grass and close my eyes. I imagine how it might have been, twenty-five hundred years ago, listening to the Buddha teach. I can almost hear his voice, floating down through the ages. It sounds like the voice of Goenka.

"These are the Four Noble Truths:

There is suffering.

There is a cause for suffering.

There is a way out of suffering.

This is the way to come out of suffering.

Sila: Morality

Abstain from unwholesome actions

Perform only wholesome actions.

Samadhi: Concentration

Focus the attention.

Concentrate the mind.

Panna: Wisdom

Observe yourself.

Purify the mind.

When all the negativities and impurities are removed from the mind, you will understand the Law of Nature, the *Dhamma*, The Ultimate Truth."

There is a stirring in the grass nearby. I open my eyes. A squirrel is racing across the lawn. A young Indian couple is standing by the *stupa*. The bus is waiting at the street.

I ride back to Benares in the colors of sunset. Along with me I bring the peacefulness I had come to the park at Sarnath to find, and much more: a resolution to follow the path of *Dhamma* that I have begun to walk, so that I may grow in wisdom and help others find their way to freedom.

Still calm inside as I get off the bus in town, I join the throngs in an evening stroll down to the Ganges. Manikarnika *ghat*, the chief cremation center on the holiest river in India, is busy. It is believed that open-air cremation is essential to the liberation of the soul after death.

Corpses, wrapped in white silk or linen, are brought through the narrow streets on bamboo stretchers and then stacked up to wait their turn on the smoking pyres. Floating ash fills my eyes, nose and mouth, and the smell of charred remains wafts through the hazy air.

Although I have heard that photographing the cremation *ghat* is not allowed, I surreptitiously raise my camera and quickly click off a frame. For some reason, I feel a need to bring an image of the reality of death at one end of the spectrum home to the other. My dearest friend, a nurse in a cancer ward, will understand.

An old *sadhu* with long white hair and faded orange robes sits down next to me near the burning *ghat*. In English, he asks what has brought me to India.

My eyes well up with tears. "Something inside just told me to come."

215

He nods with understanding. "Good for you. You have listened."

He tells me he was once a college professor with a wife and children, and had all the material things he could possibly want. Now, in his old age, he is a wandering holy man, living on the charity of others, pursuing a spiritual path for the rest of his days.

As we watch the bustle of activity before us he says, "In your country, death is considered to be the opposite of life. Here in India, death is viewed as the opposite of birth. It is just one event in the continuous cycle of life, death and rebirth."

Bursts of orange flame and plumes of smoke billow up from the pyres. His voice is almost inaudible. "The body is only the vehicle. The soul is the driver."

Later that evening at my hotel I meet Ellie, a German woman about my age who is also traveling alone. She has curly red hair and an infectious laugh, and suggests that we spend the next day together. She wants to see the sunrise ritual on the Ganges, and I really want to go back again, so we make an early morning plan that does not include the regular tourist boat.

We set out for the river at 5:00 a.m. The humidity already has my thin cotton blouse sticking to my back. As we near the *ghats*, several men approach us to hire their rowboats. After a bargaining ritual, we follow one man to his boat and get in.

To our surprise, the man then gives a call, and a teenage boy gets in to row the boat, obviously leaving the man free to find more business. We soon pull up at another dock where the teenager gets out and a boy no more than five or six years old takes over the oars.

I balk at having such a little child at the helm, and speak out before we are pushed away from the dock.

"Wait just a minute. He's too small to do this job." I look at Ellie for help.

She takes up the case, and sparks seems to fly from her red hair as she reaches out to grab the arm of the older boy.

"Come back in here," she says, her German accent expressing authority. "You should be ashamed, making this little fellow row the boat all alone."

Looking sheepish, the teenager gets back in the boat and begins to row. I want them both to be in school. Yet, I know that it is not practical for them, and that they are on the path they will likely follow for the rest of their lives – working to earn a few *rupees* a day to give to the family. But today at least, the young one will have a reprieve from his lonely destiny, and looks delighted to have his brother (cousin? uncle?) share the burden and the ride.

Laughing together, the two boys take us out on the water for our surreal peek into the world of devotion and ritual at the edge of the holy river. Other small boats carry pilgrims who toss offerings of flowers and rice into the river and lean over to fill little brass jugs with the holy water. Once again I am mesmerized as the sun rises upon the ancient city and its timeless dance at the water's edge.

During the boat ride and the rest of the day that I spend with Ellie, I contemplate the friendships I have formed with the few solo travelers I have met. It is as if we have a special kinship right from the beginning, born of an inherent understanding of the challenges and rewards of being in India alone. I think it would take months in America to develop the kind of openness that characterizes these relationships. On the road, there is simply no time, nor use, for pretense.

I tell Ellie how happy her laugh makes me feel, and how much I enjoy our time together. She puts her freckled arm around my shoulders and gives me a squeeze in reply.

The day's mail brings a letter from my mother requesting that I bring her some of the silk for which she has heard Benares is famous. She wants to make a dress, or two. I am astonished. She doesn't even know how to sew. But it is the only thing she has asked for, so I feel that I have to honor the request.

I complain to Ellie that I don't know the first thing about silk, or any other fabric for that matter. We ask around and are directed to the streets of the silk vendors. Soon I am buried under bolts of material thrown at me from every direction.

After several aggravating hours I choose yardage sufficient to make two different dresses, or whatever my mother might have in mind. After the fabric is cut, the shopkeeper tells me that he does not accept Traveler's Checks, but only deals in cash. I do not have enough *rupees* on me, the banks are already closed for the day, and I am leaving by early train in the morning. I am in a panic. For some crazy reason, at that moment, bringing the silk to my mother seems like the most important mission of the whole journey.

Ellie becomes aware of my dilemma. Without a word, she reaches into the little purse she keeps inside her shirt and hands me two hundred *rupees*.

I can't believe it. I would not think of giving another traveler, especially one I am unlikely to ever see again in my life, that kind of money.

"How will I pay you back?" I protest. "I'm leaving in the morning and there's no way to get money changed before then."

"You'll be in Kathmandu next month, right?" she says. "Well, meet me in Durbar Square in front of the House of the *Kumari Devi*, The Living Goddess, on April fourth at 2:00 p.m. You can bring me the money then."

I just look at her, an unasked question in my eyes.

"I trust you," she answers.

*Understand that the body is merely
the foam of a wave, the shadow
of a shadow, and travel on.*

The Buddha

The Temple of the Singing Birds

I sit stiffly, hour after sweltering hour, crunched shoulder-to-shoulder on the packed train from Benares to Gaya. My agitation is almost more than I can bear as I cringe and bounce with every rock and roll of the train, feeling the crunch of peanut shells and other trash under my feet, nearly overwhelmed by the crush and smell of humanity.

Across the aisle from me, an Indian woman repeatedly screams out in her sleep and clutches at her crumpled sari. I wonder if some of those terrifying Hindu deities adorned with writhing snakes and human skulls are dancing madly through her dreams.

I try to focus my attention on my sensations, but my mind just wants "out of here!" I remind myself that this is only temporary, and look forward to reaching Bodhgaya tomorrow, the very place where Buddha attained enlightenment.

When the train finally pulls to a stop in Gaya at 11:00 p.m., my sense of relief is short-lived. I am trapped in the steamy coach by multitudes of people pressing to get in the very door I am trying to get out.

In desperation, I raise my duffel bag to chest level and use it as a battering ram to force a path through the wild crowd and onto the platform. I am surprised by my own ferocity, but grateful I could call up my strength when needed.

It is too late to look for a place to stay, so I curl my tired, cramped body on a wood-slat bench in the station's waiting room. Covering my eyes with a bandana to keep out the bright lights, I sleep intermittently between the noisy crackling of train announcements and the bites of hungry mosquitoes.

Bodhgaya better be worth it.

In the morning, at the ticket window, a crazy drunk man leans on me heavily. I move away, but he moves with me. When I feel his breath on my ear I decide that he is too close for comfort. I poke my elbow firmly into his stomach and say loudly, "Back off, mister." It might as well be a call to arms for every other man in the station.

In an instant, there are about twenty of them all over the guy, yelling angrily and taking turns punching him and kicking him to the ground. I watch helplessly, not knowing how to stop the onslaught. After only a few minutes, the one-sided fight is over. I feel sorry for the poor drunk, bruised and propped up in a corner, even as I salute my thanks to my "rescuers," who are busy patting each other on the back and reveling in their moment of glory. I have a feeling this incident will give them a much-needed sense of importance, and something to talk about, for a long time.

A *ricksha* takes me the few miles from Gaya to Bodhgaya and stops at the Burmese *Vihara,* the monastery where I plan to stay. I am shown to a tiny cubicle, completely barren except for a wooden plank bed. I don't know what I expected, but right now I feel too old, too tired and not devoted enough to live so austerely. Disappointed in the place, and in myself, I leave apologetically.

I slump back in the waiting *ricksha*. As the confused driver pulls me from place to place while I seek clean, comfortable accommodation, I have the sense of being on automatic pilot. Right now I feel neither brave nor cowardly, strong nor weak. The auto-pilot to survival seems to have taken over the controls, navigating from a base of information and experiences accumulated in the recent, and not so recent, past.

I find a decent space in the dormitory at the Tourist Bungalow. I want, and definitely need, a shower, but am told there is no water available anywhere in town right now.

Oh, well. Dirt is as anicca as everything else.

An aura of peace pervades Bodhgaya. The village is a melting pot of Buddhism, with a temple representing each Buddhist tradition. I visit them all.

The square, flat-roofed Tibetan temple is painted ornately in bright hues of red and blue. As I turn the prayer wheels outside, I am filled with anticipation of what awaits me in the mountains of Nepal, just a few days from now. Inside the sanctuary, a row of butter candles flickers along the altar and casts a warm glow on the Buddha's beatific smile.

Across the road, the sweeping roof lines and mosaic walls of the Thai temple are a familiar sight, evoking memories of Bangkok and the first shaky days of this journey. *Has it been two months, two moments or two lifetimes since I was there?*

In the center of town, the Mahabodhi Temple towers over everything. It looks like many of the Hindu temples in India, but this is the most important Buddhist shrine in Bodhgaya. It was built over a thousand years ago next to the tree where Buddha became enlightened. Although that tree is no longer standing, the "Bodhi Tree" which flourishes in the garden nearby is said to be a descendant of the original tree under which Buddha sat meditating twenty-five centuries ago (five hundred years before the birth of Christ), vowing not to move a muscle until he attained enlightenment.

Now that's what I call a "sitting of great determination."

In the courtyard of the Mahabodhi temple, a western girl with dark braids and dressed in Tibetan clothing performs a meditative ritual of devotional prostrations. Standing with palms together in prayer position, she raises her hands above her head and brings them back down to her chest; then she lowers her body flat to the ground and lies face down for a moment before rising to her feet. Palms together again, she repeats the pattern smoothly over and over in a continuous flow. I sit quietly nearby and watch her for about half an hour, wondering about her motivation. There is no way to know how long she has been here, and as I leave she shows no signs of stopping.

I later learn from another western pilgrim that a devotee of Tibetan Buddhism must perform 100,000 of these ritual prostrations as part of that particular path to enlightenment. I think it must take years to do them all, but I am fascinated by the idea. I can almost imagine myself doing this practice.

My final stop is the Japanese temple, a low structure built of natural wood and shoji screens. The Zen garden by the entrance is like a small ocean of flowing gravel which has been carefully raked into swirling patterns around occasional islands of stone. This temple quickly becomes my favorite in Bodhgaya, because the sanctuary is filled with little singing birds that nest and thrive in two great golden trees, one on each side of the altar. Their darting movements cause the leaves to shimmer in the candlelight. What a beautiful place to live. I consider the possibility of staying here forever.

As I sit cross-legged on the floor and watch the black-robed monk perform the mid-morning offering ceremony, I envision myself at home in the small compound which surrounds the temple of the singing birds. It makes me feel very happy.

When the *puja* is over, a monk of slight build, in orange robes and shaven head, approaches me with sparkling eyes, and reaches out to take my hand. Suddenly I realize that the monk is a young Asian woman, a Buddhist nun. She leads me outside, where we laughingly discover that we cannot understand a single word of each other's language. But it doesn't seem to matter.

Beckoning me into her small room in the nunnery next to the temple, she motions for me to sit down on her plank bed, peels oranges and makes tea for us. How sweet she is, how open and warm, how clear her eyes. It would be wonderful to be able to converse with her, to ask her why she chose to become a nun and what it feels like to live her life the way she does. Instead we share fruit and tea and giggles, and I wonder if somehow she knew that I was drawn to living here, and that's why she invited me to visit her room.

As I prepare to leave, she points to my camera and herself, and I understand that she would like me to take her photograph so that I will not forget her. She sits down on the steps of the temple, folds her legs beneath her, rests her hands softly in her lap and closes her eyes, assuming an attitude of *samadhi*, or deep concentration. I take the picture, and then capture one of her infectious grin with my camera as well.

As we bow *Namaste'* and wave good-bye, I realize that I didn't get her name; but I know I will not forget her face, or the feeling of her joy, bubbling up from deep within her and splashing me playfully.

In the afternoon, I walk across the river to where a *stupa*, a small Buddhist shrine, sits in a tangle of high grass and weeds. The quote on its stone face compares the action of meditating to that of a brass smith polishing away the discoloration of tarnish on the original self. I find it a nicer image than my analogy of "dumping the garbage." Perhaps tarnish is more like what actually accumulates than trash, just dulling the original shine, the true nature of the self.

I'm convinced now that I have never stopped shining underneath; it's just that the air of existence, of life, has taken its toll. The longer the tarnish accumulates, the harder it may be to clean, but with a bit of effort – awareness plus equanimity – ding! I think the brightness of the shine can be renewed.

I return to the Japanese temple as the light of the day begins to wane and the air cools. I do not see the little nun, but her bright presence is there for me. I wonder how I would look in shaven head and nun's robes, and whether any other way exists in this world for me than the kind of earthly life I have known. I feel drawn to living the life of a renunciate, a devotee; and then I chuckle to myself.

228

Yesterday you wouldn't even consider sleeping on the plank bed in the Burmese Vihara! Now you're going to shave your head? Ha! Better you stick to watching your sensations for now and remembering the truth of impermanence.

Meditating to the songs of the temple birds, I realize that while I will continue to strive for balance and awareness in my life, I do not crave "enlightenment," or any particular spiritual goal. I also become aware that I am no longer haunted by the past nor obsessed with the future. Everything I am experiencing in the moment is perfect and enough. With that acceptance, I feel relieved of a burden, and much lighter inside.

Hmmm. Is that, indeed, what en"light"enment is about?

Seeking means: to have a goal;
but finding means: to be free,
to be receptive, to have no goal.

Hermann Hesse

Hello Nepal, Goodbye Heart

Phan tas ma go' ria (n) 1: a complex scene that constantly changes, whose images may be real or imagined.   2: Kathmandu.

Like a living prism, the city of Kathmandu catches a single light moment in time and breaks it into a million vibrating light moments, each one projecting a rainbow of kaleidoscopic patterns which fluctuate in rapid succession. Often I have to look twice to know whether what appears before my eyes really exists, or is some hallucinatory vision from the outer limits of my mind.

The streets are a swirling stream of handsome women in bright, flowing *saris* and dark Tibetan dresses; serious men in white clothing sporting small, square, patterned caps on their heads; long-lashed, laughing children playing tag in dirty rags; wild-eyed *sadhus* in tattered loincloths; shaven-haired monks in crimson robes; strolling bovines and starving dogs; playful monkeys and pathetic beggars.

Twisting, narrow lanes meander in every direction, punctuated by mud holes, garbage, and cow dung. Odors waft from every doorway, filling the air with curry, incense and apple pie. Vendors set up stalls in every available space, selling all manner of goods from used flashlight batteries to intricately detailed Tibetan religious paintings. Small Hindu figures on corner shrines wear garlands of orange flowers and dots of red powder on their foreheads.

The enormous all-seeing eyes of the Great Compassionate Buddha stare down at me from atop the temple at Swayambunath. Carved wooden friezes on the pagodas of Durbar Square depict erotic tableaus from Hindu mythology. The twelve-year-old girl chosen as the "Living Goddess" gazes down wistfully from the window of the ancient building in which she is enshrined. (There I find Ellie, as promised. We happily hug and briefly catch up, and I pay her back the money I borrowed in Varanasi. "I knew I could trust you!" she chirps.)

 Stoned drug users wander aimlessly along Freak Street, followed by dealers touting hashish and cocaine. Tibetan Buddhist devotees circumambulate the great *stupa* at Bodanath, spinning hand-held prayer wheels and chanting in low, gutteral voices. Smoke rises lazily from the cremation *ghat* on the Bagmati River, which flows into the Mother Ganges.

And through it all, the tinkling of bicycle bells and the ding-dong of temple bells call me to attention, call me to prayer, call me to be aware of the changing nature of every moment, aware of the impermanence of everything I see, everything I feel, everything I think, everything I am.

Kathmandu!

234

I hail a taxi outside the intimate, friendly Kathmandu Guest House where I stayed my first night in town. They have a lovely garden, and the sweet smell of jasmine perfumes the air. I will miss the garden, but I am ready for the greater adventures which await me.

"Yellow Pagoda Hotel. How much?" I ask the driver.

He points to the meter on the dashboard in reply. I nod okay, put my duffel bag on the seat and climb in.

When we arrive, the driver says, "Forty *rupees*."

I look at the meter. It hasn't moved from zero.

"What do you mean, forty *rupees*?" I challenge him. "That's not what the meter says. I agreed to pay by the meter."

He shrugs his shoulders. "Meter not working" are the only words he chooses to say in English.

It's not worth an argument, but I won't fall for his ploy. I hand him twenty-five, which is probably still too much, and enter the lobby. This is where I am to meet the people with whom I will spend the next three weeks trekking in the Himalayas.

I booked space on the upcoming trek around Annapurna before I left California. I knew I was not prepared to take on 23 days of difficult walking, 22 nights of camping at high altitude and crossing an 18,000' snow covered mountain pass entirely by myself. But having companions for a while will not make this journey any less solo, just less solitary.

I am given a room key and instructions to be back in the lobby at 7:00 p.m. There our group convenes for orientation. We are five men and five women. Seven of us are from California. We are each traveling alone. No couples, no friends, no "baggage."

The men: William, a teacher; Rob, an airline pilot; Richard, a businessman; Cal, an engineer; and Derek, a sea captain (red beard and all).

The women: Janet, an attorney; Beth, a student; Joanna, a clinical psychologist; Laura, a psychotherapist; and me (no label).

Our trek leader and guide is Jesse, a bushy-haired, fresh-faced California transplant to Nepal via the Peace Corps several years ago. Karma Sherpa, round and smiling, will be in charge of our many porters.

Each of us has individual goals and reasons for being here. Yet we quickly accept that we are in this together. The forthcoming trek will be challenging and occasionally dangerous. I sense that the quality of our bonding in the days ahead could profoundly affect the upcoming journey for each of us.

This is real now. Kathmandu. The Himalayas. Shangri-La. Living my dreams. Creating my life. My skin is covered with goose bumps.

Trekking Notes - Day 1

ek – one
dui – two
tin – three
chaar – four
panch – five
namaste' – hello, goodbye

At 6:00 a.m. we meet in the hotel restaurant for breakfast. A mini-bus arrives soon after and transports us to the town of Dumre, where we will begin our trek into the mountains.

I share the two-hour ride with Beth, a college student who is listed to be my tent-mate. At twenty-four years old, she is the youngest of the group.

During the ride Jesse gives us some general information.

"Nepal is a Hindu Kingdom with a Buddhist heart - a blend of religious cultures living together in harmonious co-existence."

He also gives us some basic instructions.

"Be sure to bury your toilet paper or put it in a plastic bag. And never ever go out at night without your flashlight."

Aside from that, and a gentle reminder to remain sensitive to the culture and environment we are visiting (invading?), there doesn't seem to be much structure or form. I like that.

The sky is clear and the first day's walk of about ten miles is on fairly even ground, following the west bank of the Marsyandi Khola. The lush river valley is heavily planted with rice in gracefully sculptured terraces which seem to cascade down the hillsides. There are no mountains in sight yet. I long to see them, to be in them.

What do I think I will find there, anyway?

We pass through a couple of small villages, which appear to be populated only by dirty children with dirty babies tied to their backs. We later discover the parents and older siblings working in nearby fields preparing to harvest the rice.

The locals on the trail are friendly, if somewhat bemused by us in our variety of trekking outfits: a conglomeration of hiking boots and running shoes, trousers and knickers, skirts and shorts, blouses, t-shirts and cut-off sweatshirts, topped off by wide-brimmed hats, baseball caps, bandanas, a beret and an assortment of dark glasses.

237

Our daypacks are the only burdens we have to carry on the trail, containing drinking water, sweater, camera, etc. The barefoot porters move ahead of us with quick, sure steps, bending beneath heavy loads overflowing with tents, cooking pots and duffle bags. Each porter carries a cone-shaped basket on his back which is supported by a wide strap across the forehead. Their laughter, chatter and high-pitched harmonious songs float back down the path to those of us trailing behind. Arriving at the planned campsite ahead of us, they set up the tents, prepare tea for the weary arrivals, and then cook *dal bhat*, the standard fare of rice and lentils, plus vegetables for dinner.

At first I feel guilty about this royal treatment, but accept that this is how it's done in Nepal. At least the porters and cooks have good jobs, and some of them also have beautiful names, like Bhakta Raj: Devotee King, and Chandra Prakash: Moon Bright. Their light spirits are a joy to have along.

As evening falls, and Beth and I settle down in our tent for the night, my body feels the fatigue of the miles and my thoughts race through the experiences of the day. Then a deep sense of personal accomplishment and satisfaction begins to flow through me. Creating both a physical and mental sensation, it provides an inner massage to my well-worked legs and a soothing lullaby to my excited mind.

Day 2

> *ram ro chha* – it is good
> *mitho chha* – it is good (referring to food)
> *na ram ro* – not good
> *chhaina* – no
> *holaa* – maybe

In the early morning at our first camp outside the village of Tortorre, I am warmed by a breakfast of steaming porridge and hot tea. Some easy stretches help ease overnight stiffness, and soon the camp is packed up and we are ready to go.

The terrain during the day climbs slightly and the mountains are disappointingly obscured by haze. I look forward to gaining altitude and being close to the peaks.

In the meantime, I discover that trekking in Nepal is nothing like hiking in the wilderness areas of America. The Himalayas are anything but a wilderness.

Tiny villages dot the hillsides and local residents travel the dirt paths by foot daily. We stop in small tea shops along the way, creating delightful breaks in the day. These stops provide the best opportunity to visit and communicate (after a fashion) with people in each village, who seem to accept us with good humor.

Jesse does the interpreting, but we are all beginning to learn some valuable words and expressions, such as *Ke garne*? ("What to do?"). This is said with a shrug of the shoulders and a tilted head, and appears to be a useful filler. I still hold that communication without words is the purest kind. Smiles and eyes tell the greatest stories.

I am impressed by Jesse's knowledge of the Nepali people, their culture and their language, as well as his patience with all of us as we ply him with questions and share our concerns. His relaxed attitude and innocent demeanor belie the depth of his knowledge and experience. I think he will be an interesting person to get to know over these next few weeks.

Highlights of the day: the great swimming hole under the wobbly suspension bridge; sunlit terraces of wheat, millet and rice making patchwork patterns on the steep hillsides; hordes of village children who know how to say "give me one pen please" and not how to wipe their noses; *rostis* for lunch (potato pancakes stuffed with diced onions, carrots, celery and cabbage); and the good company.

The group is meshing nicely, and except for the giant black ants, it's wonderful so far.

I'm feeling more balanced lately. The mind games of rummaging around in the past, worrying about the future, questioning every decision and fueling self-doubt have practically disappeared.

Right now I'm just so glad to be here, to be aware, to be alive.

The road uphill
and the road downhill
are one and the same.

Heraclitus

A Moment of Silence

Day 3

dinos – give me please
chiyaa – tea
khaanaa – food, meal
dudh – milk
tato paani – hot water
chiso paani – cold water
raksi – home made spirits
pugyo – enough

A long, hot, dry day and a slow uphill grind. The personal challenge of crossing a decrepit wooden bridge over a deep, narrow gorge. The excitement of seeing the tips of white-capped mountains ahead.

Feels like well over ten miles to me as I arrive exhausted at our encampment in Philesangu. Approaching the camp from the hillside above, our bright orange tents glow in the twilight like smiling jack-o-lanterns against the rich green backdrop of the terraces all around. A welcome sight at the end of the day.

Each of us in the group is discovering our own pace, and I find that I can walk alone for long stretches without even seeing anyone else. I enjoy the freedom of not having to conform to a particular schedule, except for showing up at mealtime, and I suppose even that is by choice. And since we have each come here alone, as individuals, there is a general appreciation for the subtle movements in and out of conversations as we share the trail.

I am realizing this will be a long, hard journey, as we head toward the goal of the *Thorung La* mountain pass at 17,790'. Here's my chance to get as strong outside as I have become inside.

Day 4

> *kalam* – pen
> *sisaa kalam* – pencil
> *kitaab* – book
> *kaapi* – notebook
> *jholaa* – shoulder bag
> *khalti* – pocket

I did not sleep well and have some painful blisters, but the morning brings a surprise as sunrise gives us our first really clear view of the peaks. The soft "alpenglow" on *Lamjung Himal* (21,000') warms my body and soul as the rising sun begins to warm the day. The weather is cooling in the evening and morning as we gain a little altitude. We have also had lots of thunder, but very little rain.

As we sit around the cooking fire in one of the small tea huts along the trail, the *didi* (literally, elder sister) makes us popped corn and tea. Some of our group drinks *chang*, the local brew of fermented barley. I stick to *chiya* (tea).

It's tough to get going again after these relaxing interludes, and the afternoon walk is always slower for me.

Today we hear from some other trekkers that three climbers with another group were killed in an avalanche. We all shudder, and share a moment of silence, knowing that even though we will not be climbing peaks of the same degree of difficulty, there is surely an element of danger in our own journey into these mountains. Any one of us could fall off the edge of the steep trail, suffer from altitude sickness, break a bone or experience some other injury. When the time comes to cross the *Thorung La*, even avalanche danger will be present.

William (the teacher) always has his way of cheering things up, though. He strums his ukulele and leads us in a sing-a-long, then hands the instrument to one of the ever-present Nepali children as he pulls a bamboo flute from his daypack and begins to play that.

I wasn't sure about William at first, an unsophisticated, childlike man who seemed to fit the least comfortably into the group. Now, I like him the best. His refreshing personality and music are a joy to have along, and he is like a Pied Piper to all the children who find us a great curiosity anyway.

Each of us in the group expresses our interest in being here in our own way. Various books, maps, compasses and star charts have appeared. William is now reading aloud from *Annapurna* by Maurice Herzog about a nine-man French expedition which climbed Annapurna in 1950. The fire is blazing brightness on our small terrace, one among thousands of terraces which have been sculpted into the hillsides over many centuries.

As William hands the book to Beth for her turn to read, it occurs to me that we're becoming a family. Lots of concern for one another, lots of sharing of information, lots of teasing and friendly banter. As if we had all known each other for a long time.

I don't know if this is typical for a group thrown together, especially in a challenging situation where cooperation is required; but I do feel very confident that we will take care of each other if problems arise, and that we will all rejoice together when we are successful.

It also begins to feel like an "expedition." Group spirit is something I haven't experienced for a long time, and never to this degree with a bunch of new people. A common bond, a common interest, a common goal. One of the most pleasant human sensations I've ever known.

Janet reads next, then Cal. Strange, I feel a certain affection already for each of them. My small mention of it brings laughter, maybe a little embarrassment. I wonder how each of them really feels about it. Not so differently than I do, I would bet.

Day 5

aamaa – mother
baa – father
sabajai – grandmother
chhoraa – son
chhori – daughter
saathi – friend

From our camp at Bondanda, we follow a very steep uphill trail through the Marsyandi River gorge to Jagal. The hardest haul yet, and particularly draining for me. Huffing and puffing, red-faced, heart palpitating. Not a good feeling.

It doesn't take much gentle urging from observant Jesse to convince me to give my backpack to the porter Chandra and put up a big black umbrella to shield myself from the intense sun. Their concern is sincere and I feel safe in their care and protected under their watchful eyes. Still, there is always the pressure to go on.

The *chang* shop where we stop for our break is sparkling clean. The *didi,* with her proud Tibetan face, is probably a wealthy woman by local standards. Around her neck hangs a grand necklace of large turquoise and coral stones, and her shining copper and metal cooking pots are displayed neatly on a freshly dusted shelf. Best of all, her roasted corn with ground chili pepper is the tastiest yet. A lovely mid-morning stop.

At lunch our cook prepares French toast. But I am too tired to eat. I just want to soak my feet and close my eyes.

Beautiful birds, butterflies, waterfalls and canyons buoy my spirits in the afternoon, but not my body. I am drained, and I've developed a case of laryngitis that doesn't help.

On arrival at our camp near the village of Chanje, I do a little laundry and hang it on a line. A few hours later, black clouds gather quickly above and drench the campsite.

As the rain pours down, all the women huddle in one tent and have a "ladies' group." We end up saying very little about ourselves and a lot about our impressions of the men.

Janet: "That camera with the huge lens that Richard always wears around his neck looks like an extra manly appendage."

(Laughter.)

Beth: "William is certainly a character isn't he?"

Joanna: "That's exactly what I like about him!"

In the end, the consensus is that they are all pretty decent guys, especially Jesse, who wins the prize for being "just too darned cute."

Heavy drops continue to fall as we head for our own tents for the night. Rainy weather tends to make me feel melancholy. My dripping clothes hang sorrowfully on the line as a testimony to my mood.

I realize that I want to be strong, but I don't want to be tough. I identify with the anxiety of Laura as she struggles to stay ahead on the trail so that she won't be left behind. But that doesn't matter to me now. It is okay to arrive last.

It's been a difficult and wonderful day. And William is still my favorite. If only I had a movie camera with sound. He deserves to be preserved.

Day 6

tapaaiko naam ke ho? – what's your name?
timi kati barsha bhayau? – how old are you?
tapaai kahaa basnuhunchha? – where do you live?
kati bajho? – what time is it?
bujhdina – I do not understand
nepali bolnu sakdina – I do not speak Nepali

The morning is punctuated by the sight of the first bright red rhododendrons which decorate these mountains in profusion during the spring months, and we lunch on cauliflower, hard boiled eggs and *chaps* (little fried puffies of

248

mashed potatoes).

At our tea stop in the village of Tal (5400' and gaining), a grimy three-year-old suckles at her Mama's breast while Mom grinds peppers and onions with mortar and pestle to add to our roasted popcorn.

The man of the house sits in the corner, reading Tibetan scriptures and chanting prayers. He pays us no mind.

When group discussion over *chiya* and *chang* turns to stories of lives back home, Richard asks me about my plans for when I return to America. I don't like being reminded, and the question makes me uncomfortable. Stumbling through a list of possibilities, I finally admit that I have no idea what will come next.

I haven't really thought about "the future" lately, being more concerned with getting where I'm going each day. It seems that this place, this moment, is all there is to my life.

Later at camp, I meditate and write by the riverside before dinner. Across the water is Bagarchhap, the most beautiful village I have ever seen. Neat, orderly and tightly packed against a green hillside.

The stone buildings have flat roofs which are piled high with firewood. Against the houses lean what I call "dugout" ladders, because the steps have been carved out of a log. According to Jesse, this is the first village on the trek with typical Tibetan architecture, common in the Manang District which we have now entered. At his suggestion, we visit the *gompa,* the Buddhist temple, in the upper part of the village.

As we walk through the great wooden door, I have to adjust my eyes to the dim light inside. The walls are painted in bright hues, and a vertical cylinder of colorful fabrics sewn together reaches from ceiling to floor. Hanging from silken cords are several cracked and faded *thankas*, the intricately detailed cloth paintings portraying the life of Buddha and other Buddhist stories. Long, narrow prayer books in Tibetan script are stacked neatly in cubbyholes. Small yak-butter candles flicker on the altar.

I am in awe. Not only of the *gompa*, but of the feelings swirling around inside me. There is something about the place which touches me deeply, strikes that lost, wailing chord somewhere in my innermost being. As if this is the very place that called to me when first I felt the attraction to the Himalayas, so many years ago; and that by being here I have answered the call, have found my Shangri-La, and have been shown the purpose of the journey. I feel as if I have come to my true home.

Being in the *gompa,* I know that I need go no farther. I have done exactly what I wanted to do, and feel the fulfillment of every desire I have ever had. If my life were to end now, I would die happily.

Everything I experience from this moment forward will be a bonus.

Adventure is not in the guidebook;
Beauty is not on the map

Terry and Renny Russell

Om! Mani Padme Hum!

Day 7

ek chhin parkhnos — wait a minute
malaai bhok laagyo — I'm hungry
bajaar — market
tyo ke ho? — what's that?
yo kati ho? — how much is this?
mahango — expensive

My spirit may be flying, but my body definitely remains earthbound. I feel as if I am being pressed to the ground by the increasing altitude, and the climb from 7100' to 9000' makes my hiking shoes feel more like balls and chains than boots. Still, since the visit to the *gompa* last evening, each measured step I take today feels like a gift.

I wonder what's going on at home.

Waterfalls thunder alongside the trail, maple trees sprout new red leaves, wild cannabis plants and crimson rhododendrons spring up around every corner. The snowy mountain views are crystal clear, creating a stark backdrop for the graceful flight of a long-winged Himalayan griffen.

253

When a large herd of goats suddenly appears and overruns the narrow path, we hug the trail edge closely, grabbing for any bush or rock so as not to be knocked down by the onrush. As the dust settles, a young Nepali goatherd appears, coaxing a stray with a gentle song and a firm stick. He greets us with a broad smile and then laughingly points his stick up to the branch of a nearby tree, where William perches precariously above the trail.

"Any port in a storm!" he calls out, before tumbling into our waiting arms.

In the afternoon we reach a fork in the trail. Nearby is a police check post where our trekking permits are examined. The check post controls access to the Nar-Phu Valley, beyond which lies Tibet. That politically sensitive region is closed to foreigners, and the officials are there to make sure we do not stray off the trail to Annapurna. Jesse handles all the paperwork.

As we walk past the trail to the forbidden valley, I feel an inner pull, as if being drawn toward the tall, rocky outcroppings guarding the valley entrance. I stop and contemplate the path, sensing a connection to the feeling I experienced in the Bagarchap *gompa*. It is vague, just an amorphous swirling within me, until I realize that the feeling is one of yearning, of longing to walk down that forbidden path until I am out of view beyond the rocks and on my way to Tibet.

Jesse comes up behind me with a soft touch on my arm. I look back at him. He has taken off his baseball cap, and the ends of his blonde curly hair shine like a halo in the sunlight. His eyes are full of understanding and caring.

"I'm sorry. It's time to go."

I sigh deeply, reluctantly turning away from the path of my heart's desire, feeling so near, yet so far away.

But from what?

In the evening there is some tent shuffling as William and Joanna decide to move in together. Other friendships are also beginning to take form, but no other romantic liaisons yet, although Janet and I tease each other about the possibilities. We both have eyes for Jesse.

As the fire begins to wane, red-bearded Derek, the sea captain, sits down next to me. He is an endearing man, and we have fun together.

"Thanks for being behind me today," I smile, mildly embarrassed by the fact that he had firmly held onto my rear end to keep me from sliding backwards down a steep embankment.

"I assure you, the pleasure was all mine," he teases. Then his face becomes serious. "I guess each of us in this group has our own reasons for being here. For me, it's the physical challenge of these mountains. What is it for you?"

"I suppose you could call it a spiritual journey for me."

He looks at me. "Your spirit seems in pretty good condition already."

"Well, so does your body. Yet you have come here to challenge its perceived limitations, and to see what possibilities lie beyond them, right?"

He nods in agreement, and a slow smile of understanding washes over his face as he gazes into the glowing coals.

As I prepare for bed, I think about my own physical challenges on this trek, and how I will meet them. The altitude of the upcoming *Thorung-La* pass is nearly 18,000'. It is a steep climb of 3000' up from the base camp, followed immediately by a 5000' knee-jerking descent down the other side. It should take us about eight hours, but Jesse says it took one person in a previous group thirteen hours! Do I have the stamina to do it? We also have to hope for good weather. Snow means more difficult hiking, and avalanche danger. And a big snowstorm will force us to turn back and return the way we have come. That would be a great disappointment to me.

I snuggle down in my sleeping bag. Brrrrr. It's really cold. I wish I had more carefully considered borrowing the down parka Jesse offered me earlier. Now it's time to remember: "Just observe whatever sensation arises with equanimity. *Anicca, anicca. . . .* this will also change."

Day 8

phohar – dirty
saphaa – clean
hijo – yesterday
aaja – today
bholi – tomorrow
ekdam – very much

Waking up in Chame. Sunrise pictures of Annapurna IV and Lamjung Himal. Fingers cold. Coffee hot. Where are the doughnuts? Mornings are now the hardest for walking. Hands swollen, nose running. Pushing on to gain strength and endurance. No thinking, eyes on the trail, just keep the feet moving. Lift, move, set down. Step, step, step. A good meditation.

On the way to 10,000'. Ladies with ruddy cheeks in long dark braids and Tibetan dresses sing exquisitely in high pitched voices as they walk through the village of Bradan carrying loads of wood upon their backs. At our lunch stop in a meadow just outside the village, the children present us with bouquets of wildflowers and the cooks present us with boiled potatoes in the skins with yak butter and Tibetan salt. Eating is an important part of the day, and food so familiar and tasty brings a lot of pleasure. I start choking them down so fast I get the hiccups.

The path up to camp at Pisang is a steep switchback leaving the river, but turns into a Sierra-like trail covered with pine needles thereafter. The mountain views are beautifully clear. It looks very white up there. Reports filter down from locals passing by that there is thigh-deep snow over the pass. A shiver of worry moves through my body from head to toe.

Day 9

aaitabaar – Sunday
sombaar – Monday
mangalbaar – Tuesday
budhabaar – Wednesday
bihibaar – Thursday
sukrabaar – Friday
shanibaar – Saturday

On the hillside across the river from our forest camp, Pisang looks like an Arizona Hopi Indian village shrouded in the morning mist. We have a wonderful view of Annapurna II. The weather is colder and windy; sunshine would feel nice.

My shoulders ache for the first time and my jaw is tight. I am apprehensive about what lies ahead. I am aware of an internal weariness which contrasts sharply with my external physical improvement.

We climb a steep ridge and rest at a saddle at the top. The view is expansive, taking in the broad, forested Manang Valley with Tilicho Peak at its head. In the distance we can see a new airport under construction. No doubt it will change the nature of this valley greatly. I am glad to be here now.

Manang is the epitome of a picturesque Tibetan village. I wander around peeking down narrow alleyways and into little courtyards where sleeping goats and dogs lie, children play, laundry dries, wood is stacked, and a lady descends the little notched steps of her "dugout" ladder. Upstairs, in an open loft, I can see grain spread out to dry.

The whole scene is fascinating to me. There is simply nothing to compare it to in my experience. I'm so grateful to be able to see life here, be part of life here, however removed from the realities of their days my short sojourn may be.

The rocky and arid Tibetan environment around Manang is dotted with *chortens*, stone shrines honoring Buddha. Strings of prayer flags printed with scripture fly from tall poles, carrying prayers on the wind.

We also pass free-standing walls which have been erected in the middle of the trail. They are piled high with sheets of slate and other rock which have been carved in relief with bits of scripture and the Buddhist mantra *Om! Mani Padme Hum!* Loosely translated, "Behold! The jewel in the lotus!"

Jesse explains that the act of carving the stones is like saying a prayer, or singing a hymn. So a *mani* wall is a wall of prayers. He tells us we are supposed to keep the wall to our right as we pass, moving in a clockwise direction, in accordance with the rotation of the Wheel of Life.

He also says it is common practice for travelers passing these *chortens* and *mani* walls to pick up a small stone nearby, offer it with the mantra *Om! Mani Padme Hum!* and add it to the pile to assure a safe journey.

So, I have been stopping at every little *chorten* and *mani* wall to leave a stone and say the mantra to help us along our way and deliver good weather over the *Thorung La*. The others tease me and joke about my obsession of finding the right stone to offer, but it feels important to me. I am honored to be here, and I want to cross that pass safely.

Jesse is the only one who doesn't judge me as I perform my personal ritual to create the best possible conditions for our journey. He waits for me to find my rock, even as the others move on, laughing.

"Don't worry about them," he says. "You are doing what the locals do. It is an admirable intention."

But in the evening the snow begins to gently fall in Manang village, and my prayers for clear weather over the pass may be an exercise in futility.

Day 10

    nilo – blue
    harito – green
    raato – red
    pahelo – yellow
    kaalo – black
    seto – white

What a relief it is to spend a day off the trail. It is a rest day in order to acclimatize to the altitude. I feel very spaced out and incredibly tired. Dry mouth and eyes. Lethargy. The effects of altitude.

There is a heavy cloud cover today, and it is chilly. But no snow yet. From our camp at Manang we look at the range of mountains facing us. Jesse points them out: Annapurna III, Gangapurna, Glacier Dome and Roc Noir. There is a geometric pattern of triangular shapes carved into the snow near the top of one of the peaks. How incredibly ordered is nature.

Janet produces crayons and large sheets of paper, which we use to make rubbings of *mani* stones today. I keep on placing my ritual stones on *chortens* and walls as we walk to the nearby village of Bryagu.

It is rather like a ghost town, almost devoid of life during the day. An eerie wind blows through the stones of the flat-roofed buildings, whipping the prayer flags and winding them around their poles. Even though nobody is home, I feel welcome here, as if the buildings themselves are reaching out to embrace me.

A white washed *gompa* sits high above the town, large and bright in contrast to the tightly packed brown-gray buildings that are nestled against the craggy cliffs for protection against the harshness of the elements. The disheveled and wild-eyed Tibetan caretaker pulls aside a tattered cheesecloth curtain for us to look at the golden Buddha. He is a little crazy, I think. The caretaker that is, not the Buddha.

Looking at the towering peaks all around, I feel as if I am nestled in the womb of the surrounding mountains. If I listen very carefully, I can almost hear them communicate silently yet with powerful force, to me, the growing child within.

Tomorrow is an important preparation day, and everyone is getting a bit uptight. William is uncharacteristically moody. Richard and Cal have headaches. Laura is a little snappy. Beth can barely lift her feet. In the evening I start to have problems with my stomach. These are all symptoms of the altitude, according to Jesse, and he's keeping an eye on all of us. But especially on me. Seems like he's always close by lately. I have a serious crush on him.

The pass looms ahead of us. It's too big to imagine, so I do my best to stay focused on the moment. It's cold outside, my nose never stops running, and I always have to pee.

When you have gone so far that
you can't manage one more step,
then you've gone just half the distance
that you're capable of.

Greenland proverb

Summits False and True

Day 11

(Enough with the Nepali vocabulary already!)

Leaving Manang in the early morning light, the scene below is like a stage set in a timeless play. Beneath the glacier, water buffalo plow the field of lightly fallen snow as they have for centuries. The people sing and talk and laugh together as they work, preparing for the warmer growing season ahead. They move slowly up and down the rows, turning, stooping, reaching, in a graceful dance with nature.

Watching them, I become aware of a separation within myself, feeling like a stranger in my own body. A sensation of being down there in the field with them, instead of up here on this foreign pathway.

The blueness of the icy lake contrasts with the whiteness of the glacial ice flow, and I feel as if I could fly above it all like some wild bird. In a way I am like a bird, on this path high above, moving at my own pace and at my own whim, uncontrolled by the same kinds of needs for survival as the people below.

They glance up and see me on the pathway, paying about as much attention to me as they would to any wild bird, or even less. They know that I will not fly off with the seed so diligently planted in the snow-flecked field.

Stopping for a moment further up on the trail, I am overcome with reverence for the majestic presence of the mountains so near. I realize how small we humans are in the grand scale of nature; how perfect is all creation.

Again, quietly, Jesse is there beside me. I look into his eyes and know that he knows what I am feeling. With a rush of emotion, I reach out to give him a grateful hug. Having him share the vision and appreciate the moment with me fills me with such joy. Again I realize that my time of being alone is ready to come to an end.

The day ends with a hard uphill pull and "base camp" is set up in a grassy valley at 14,500'. It is the last stop before THE PASS. The altitude continues to take its toll on me. I'm sick with nausea and stomach pain, unable to even eat dinner. I hope that none of us will have to turn back with altitude sickness, especially me.

The good news is, no sign of snow! Looks like my efforts at the *mani* walls were not in vain after all. (But did anyone thank me? Noooooo.)

I accept the offer of Jesse's warm down jacket tonight to comfort myself. There is definitely a growing affection between us, and I'm not quite sure what to do about it.

Day 12

"Pass Day"

The air is thin and the fire is difficult to light, but the porters still manage to make tea to warm us on our rest stop half way up the snow covered pass.

I look around at the group and laugh, giddy with the altitude and strain of the climb. What a sight we are! A bunch of Nose-Cote covered faces hidden by bandit bandanas, wrap-around sunglasses and hats of every kind. We're doing pretty well so far – at least we're all here. And the weather could not be more perfect.

Jesse carries my daypack for me as I continue my struggle with the altitude. He stays close by me while still keeping a careful eye on everyone else in the group.

I notice that Richard, the oldest of us in his late-forties, is moving even more slowly than I. He stops to lean on a walking stick now and then. I know how he feels. It's all I can do to put one foot in front of the other. But each time I look around, the peaks themselves seem to encourage me, inspiring me to push ahead. Every step becomes a creative effort as I climb toward an elusive summit shrouded in the misty glow of the early morning sun. It's become a meditation in movement: Step. Breathe. Step. Breathe. *Anicca. Anicca. Anicca.*

My impression is that we're like silhouettes here. Without color, without feeling, without meaning in the shadow of these larger-than-life mountains. How very important we think we are. How self-centered and small our minds.

I am humbled as my universe expands around me, including so much more in my perception of "life." Everything that exists is part of my life, as I am part of all else. It is only my thoughts which set me apart. Can I let them go? Can I become one with all that is around me? Part of a universal mind? Even my silhouette would not show then, for I would blend and breathe as one with these peaks as they sit on their mountain thrones of earthly splendor.

Dizzy from the heights, exhilarated by the magnificence, exhausted from the climb, I see a cairn on the horizon up ahead. The pile of stones is topped by a prayer flag on a stick, blowing in the wind.

It must be the summit! Oh, thank goodness. I don't think I can go a step farther.

But as I approach the landmark, I see yet another hill looming in the distance topped by another cairn, and my legs feel as if they will give way beneath me. I start to sit down on the crunchy snow, but before my body comes in contact with the ground a strong arm pulls me back up.

"Don't stop now," says Jesse. "You're almost to the top. Keep the momentum or it will be even more difficult to go on."

I marvel at the ease with which he moves in the altitude. He reminds me of a bird flying lightly through these mountains with the confidence of wings.

After the frustration of several more "false" summits, the true crest of the pass comes into view, marked by a huge cairn and many prayer flags flapping in the wind. The Sherpas and most of the other members of the group have arrived and cheer me on. I feel a rush of adrenaline as I push the last few euphoric steps to the top, where I am greeted with handshakes, hugs and kisses of congratulations and camaraderie.

A sudden flow of tears provides a welcome relief from the stress of the ascent as I place a final rock on the stone cairn marking the true summit, in grateful thanks for a safe journey.

But I am soon reminded that it is not over yet, and we may not linger at the top for more than the time it takes to catch our breath and drink some water. We must reach the base of the mountain before the cloak of darkness closes in and envelopes us.

And so the hours, the agony, it has taken to reach the summit, dissolve in time and space. A goal which seemed so real, took so much energy, becomes simply another landmark on the map of my life. Nothing to hold on to. Impermanent. Changing. The truth of *anicca*.

There is only this moment. And this one. And . . . anything else is a "false summit."

On the journey is the only place to be.

At high altitudes, there's no place for the fantastic, because reality itself is more marvelous than anything man could imagine.

Rene Daumal

Time is in the Mind of the Observer

We begin the long descent of 5000' through scree and snow, trying to keep the knees loose and the balance stable on the steep, slippery surface. But going downhill is comparatively easy, and we sing songs from the sixties and laugh as we dance toward the shadowy mystical mountains of Dolpo and Mustang in the distance ahead.

Arriving at the campsite in Muktinath about 4:00 p.m., I pull off my boots, stretch myself out on the ground, and gaze at the perfect blueness of the sky at 12,500' in the Himalayas of Nepal.

I have just traversed a Himalayan pass which is higher than any mountain in the Continental United States, and by the end of this trek I will have walked over 200 miles.

I am an integral part of a cohesive and supportive group of people who, striving together, reached a common goal.

My cells are vibrating with a sense of pride and accomplishment, and I do not deny myself the pleasure.

273

Day 13

A rest day in Muktinath is welcomed by all. In the late morning we put bathing suits on under our clothes and walk to the Hindu temple up the hill. There are 108 waterspouts, each carved in the shape of a bull's head, continually flowing with holy water which is believed to cleanse one's sins on earth. We strip off our jeans and shirts and run through the freezing water, whooping with the shock of the cold. Don't know about my sins, but every pore of my body tingles with aliveness, awareness and pure joy at being clean again.

The lazy afternoon is punctuated by friendly bargaining and trading with the local merchants who spread their wares out on old Tibetan blankets near our campsite. The women sit and spin wool while we negotiate. One of my old blouses for two yak hair scarves. A few dollars for a small string of turquoise and coral beads.

A wonderful thing about the Nepali people: they are always smiling! I cannot know what jokes they are thinking in their heads, nor what fun they may be making of me. They simply seem so happy all of the time, as if there really is nothing to worry about in life at all. Many of them do not even know if there will be enough food for tomorrow. But why worry? Does that help? Perhaps that is really what they do know – that worry is useless, and they will either eat or they won't. They will live and they will die. Both of these things will happen in the course of their lives, and are accepted equally as the truth. So why worry? It is all *anicca*.

In the evening we have a party in the local tavern, a ramshackle building with rough-hewn wooden tables and benches. Porters, locals and trekkers together singing, dancing and drinking *raksi*, the local brew.

During one particularly liberated dancing moment, Jesse raises his arms high in the air and shouts to all of us with a big grin: "*This* is trekking!"

Later, as he and I wander back to camp in the crisp, starry darkness, our hands reach out and touch, grab hold, and a moment later we are in each other's arms. He asks if I will spend the night in his tent "just to be close, nothing else." It is what I want, too.

We zip open the flap and lay down beside each other with our heads poking outside to gaze at the star-studded Himalayan sky. In the happiness we feel at being together, it isn't long before "just being close" becomes tender kissing and soft caresses. Soon we close the flap behind us and snuggle together in sweet intimacy.

It feels so good not to be alone any more.

Day 14

In the early morning mist, the small village of Jharkot sits quietly among ghostly barren trees. I photograph a snow-capped mountain reflected in a still pool. It is the first of many reflections for me today, in more ways than one. The mood of the rest of the group seems quiet and reflective, too. We reached our peak, and it's all downhill from here.

A long dry road brings us to an overlook. Below is an abandoned village which was apparently destroyed by a landslide. The skeletons of buildings and a faded patchwork of dried-up fields reflect the impermanence of all things and tell silent stories of lifetimes gone by.

A short time later, high atop the hill approaching the village of Kagbeni, the eerie sound of a distant drum wafts through the wind. It seems to be coming from the town nestled far below. Stone houses with flat Tibetan roofs are surrounded by neatly arranged bright green terraced fields. Caves have been carved out of the face of the mountain above the village.

My brows knit together in puzzlement and my shoulders hunch up of their own accord. There stirs in me a feeling so vague, a sense of remembering so amorphous, I can't even begin to identify it; but my body reacts by remaining tense as we descend the hillside to the village.

I wander through the narrow cobbled streets in a trance, mesmerized by the hypnotic beat of the invisible drum, feeling literally fragmented. I have the strange sensation that pieces of me are everywhere, stuck on the low rock walls, the flat stone buildings, the carved wooden window frames. It is a strong feeling now – the feeling of having been here before, of knowing this village.

Finally, I gain the courage to express my confusion, my puzzlement, my sense of fragmentation to the others.

Cal says, "Maybe you were a Tibetan princess in a previous life." Then Joanna pipes up, "Is that a prerequisite to being a Jewish Princess?" They all laugh, but I can't shake the *deja vu*.

As we leave the village my head is spinning. Is there truth in the idea of past lives? Is that why I have been drawn so strongly to this part of the world?

At our lunch stop, the new closeness between Jesse and me is apparent. Derek notices Jesse's hand resting on my knee and he looks away. *Is he disappointed?* Janet sees our arms

276

touching and her eyes darken. *Is she jealous?* No one else shows any outward reaction, but I am uncomfortable, imagining the judgments of the rest of the group.

I wonder if I have made a big mistake. I feel guilty.

In my self-consciousness, I move away from Jesse. He looks at me with a question in his eyes, not understanding. I have to decide if my feelings for him are stronger than my discomfort.

The trail takes us through the Kali Gandaki River gorge, the deepest in the world. The river is narrow here, but there is an exciting power in the immensity of the gorge and in the interminable battering winds. Jesse and I walk together, and the gorge seems to swallow us up as we look for fossils and hold hands for stability against the gusts. I arrive in Jomsom feeling raped by the wind and exhausted from the emotions of the day.

Snug in my tent as darkness falls, I wonder how one can experience this place, the magical, mystical Himalaya, this frozen moment in time, and then go "home" and resume one's previous life. The effect upon me is so profound, it is frightening.

This is another world, and mine will never be the same again.

Day 15

As we leave the snow and altitude behind, we are greeted by fields of waving oats and wheat shimmering in the sun. A shepherd plays a haunting flute to his flock on the hillside. The floating notes of the piper seem to move through my heart and send waves of sensation throughout my being.

Stopping in the white-washed stone village of Marpha for a glass of their special peach *chang* and a plate of apple pancakes provides a lovely interlude. It is difficult to restrain myself from reaching out to touch Jesse all the time, but I feel that we need to be more discreet, and tell him so.

Upon the invitation to permanently share his tent, I realize that I don't want to give that much. He has certainly captured my heart, but I know I still need my own space.

It is the "down" side now, and we are on the way back. No matter how hard I try to ignore that, it causes me to feel melancholy. The summit has been reached, and the circle now takes us back to Kathmandu. I've thought when I get home and am asked the inevitable question, "What will you do now?" I'll say, "Go back to Nepal." I can't imagine being anywhere but here right now. Each day falls gently into place, past and future have lost their meaning, and time – the measure of reality – has lost its cohesiveness, the very reason for which the concept of "time" was created.

Day 16

This morning as we leave Larjung I point to some dark areas high on a nearby cliff wall, and ask Jesse, "What are those little holes way up there in the side of the cliff?"

"Those are ancient meditation caves in which Buddhist monks would sit in contemplation for long periods of time. Food was raised up to them by ropes."

The weird feeling courses through my body again. "Can we go up there?"

"Let's go."

Jesse and I move ahead of the others, turning off the main trail below the caves. The path is very steep, not really a path at all. We scratch and claw our way up through loose dirt and tree roots. At one point, I am ready to give up, feeling suddenly tired and ill. I decide it's not worth the effort.

"Come on, I'll help you." Jesse extends a strong arm down for me to grab hold.

With a final push up over the edge onto the floor of the cave, I look around at a place that feels very familiar to me, like a home away from home.

But I have never been in any place like this in my life.

The rock walls are carved out into a cozy niche with room to meditate and sleep; a small charred area in the corner identifies the cooking fire; and the view through the craggy opening is breathtaking. Majestic mountains span the horizon and line the immense river gorge, while the whitewashed *gompa* sits peacefully on a low hill surrounded by fields in every shade of green.

All I want to do is stay here for a long, long time.

Jesse and I sit quietly, gazing at the timeless scene below, until the voices of Janet and Cal can be heard approaching the cave. With their arrival, the spell is broken, and I emerge into the present again. I finally understand what Albert Einstein meant when he said, *"The only real time is that of the observer, who carries with him his own time and space."*

After sliding back down the hill, walking feels like a chore and my breathing is shallow. I am extremely tired, and I know that my resistance to returning to "civilization," especially America, is wearing me out, too.

I'm concerned about my growing dependency on Jesse and my increasing self-consciousness about my performance on the trail. I don't think he judges me, but I watch my nagging self-critic begin to emerge once more. Can it be true that being

279

with a man again will undermine the personal strength I have gained through being independent and alone? Is my psyche so frail as that? *I fear that it may be.*

I also notice that the group spirit has definitely changed.

The cohesiveness of an expedition has deteriorated into a fragmented bunch of individuals who are experiencing the aftermath of a great high. Together, we have achieved our mutual goal, and now only the anticlimactic end of the trek lies ahead. Maybe they, too, are having difficulty imagining being anywhere but here, but they are handling it quite differently than I am.

Several people are escaping into drinking the alcoholic brews of *chang* and *raksi* during the day and are smoking lots of *bidi* cigarettes. The tenor of the group has become less reflective and more raucous, with conversations punctuated by insensitive jokes and "playful" insults. I tend to pull away from this, and find myself spending more time alone.

Maybe it's my egocentric mind at work, but I sense another undermining factor that I believe has subtly sabotaged our cohesiveness. In the beginning, we each played "follow the leader" (Jesse) through the Himalayas behind someone who treated us all equally. But along the way the game changed, and it didn't set well with some of the players. The leader had chosen a favorite.

A true journey,
no matter how long the travel takes,
has no end.

William Least-Heat-Moon

Culture Shock

Day 17

We camp below the Dhauligiri Ice Fall, a frozen flow of snow and ice tumbling like a solid river off the steep slopes, and are surrounded by almost 360 degrees of snow-capped peaks. There is some commotion at breakfast as a porter discovers that a yak appears to have fallen off a nearby cliff during the night.

Remembering our instructions on the very first day of the trek, Joanne quips, "That's what he gets for going out at night without his flashlight!"

The air is crisp as we hike up to the base of the Dhaulagiri Ice Fall at 12,500' through a lovely rhododendron forest. How beautiful is a perfect crimson rhododendron against the background of a snowy peak! Wild strawberries, purple iris, pipthanthis, viburnum – a floral arrangement unmatchable by any efforts of humankind.

The ice fall creaks and groans as it shifts and moves imperceptibly down the mountain like some massive frozen giant. William reports to us that in 1969 its deep crevasses and unpredictable movements swallowed seven members of an American expedition attempting to climb Dhauligiri. We share another moment of silence.

Perched on a land saddle near the icefall we are surrounded entirely by mountains and sky, and I feel an incredible freedom in being so high. In the stillness and beauty up there I understand why many cultures position their holy places of worship as high as possible on mountaintops or hills. It really does feel closer to God.

Day 18

Food becomes the main attraction as the peaks recede behind us. Corn bread with jam is the hit of the day in Kalopani, with fresh potato chips running a close second.

Walking alone on a forested trail, I spontaneously break into song. As my version of "Amazing Grace" floats through the trees, the birds and butterflies are my only audience, their fluttering wings my only applause. Solitude is so very precious to me, and yet I like knowing that when I am ready, it will end.

Beth has moved in with Janet, who was left alone when Joanne moved in with William. So now I have my own private tent. It is a fine place, and a good place to come back to. Room to stretch, to bathe and dress, to hear my thoughts, or not. A haven on this lovely hillside populated by cows, goats and rushing waterfalls.

I have occasional thoughts of writing my family and friends, but *Ke garne?* ("What to do?") Where would I even begin at this point? I have no desire to communicate about all of this yet. More difficult to admit, there is really nothing, and no one, that I miss.

Day 19

Walking through the narrowest part of the Kali Gandaki River Gorge today, I am fascinated by the strata of the rock walls, the violence of the rushing river, the patterns of the water churning and flowing under the bridge with no handrails. Wild cannabis and pomegranates texture the smooth canvas of a warm clear day.

The notes I made yesterday seem to have been written weeks or months ago. Time is fading and blending and melting together and the date and hour continue to lose meaning or importance. There is only the moment.

We arrive at Tatopani, which means hot water. The town is named for the hot springs that bubble up and warm the river water flowing by.

Tatopani appears to be a trekkers' hangout, with numerous shops and small hotels, entirely different from the less-traveled Manang side of the pass. But the *tato pani* in the river feels great. Jesse and I put on our bathing suits, pour plastic bowls of warm water over each other's backs, wash our hair and clothes. We lose only one sock to the current of the river.

Sitting on the bank in the early evening quiet, the two of us discuss life, love, meditation and the "future" (which doesn't go much beyond the next day or two), as we look more deeply into each other's hearts, and our own.

I admit to feelings of inadequacy, thinking I have so little to teach and so much to learn. He helps me to discover what is most important to me: to be an inspiration to others. And when he tells me that I have deeply touched his own life in that way, I feel acknowledged through all the layers of my being.

Why hasn't anyone ever seen me so clearly before?

I feel as if I have found a kindred spirit, and am grateful for the partnership.

Day 20

Have twenty days really passed? Well, today feels like about twenty in one, I'm soooo exhausted. Tatopani to Gorapani via Sikha (with a stop at Bina's Bar and Grill), and an uphill day worse for me than the pass itself.

What's going on with me?

Jesse is very sensitive to my fatigue, and thinks I may have contracted a bacterial infection or parasitic condition. He carries my pack, brings me water to wash up and serves me tea.

Though I feel too tired to even take pictures, I want to remember the images of my favorite untaken photographs today: rhododendron petals covering the path bordered by jack-on-the-pulpit, a strange orchid-like plant; the carved wooden windows on the hacienda style buildings in the village of Dana, which looks like a ghost town out of the American Old West; three girls on a porch, lined up one behind the other, industriously picking nits and lice out of each other's hair; a screaming farmer whose neighbor's cow ate his crop!

Everyone and everything in America seems a million miles away, in distance and time. Sometimes I wonder if I will ever see them again. Certainly, it will be with different eyes.

Day 21

Riots of rhododendrons line our forest way today for a lovely walk, improved by the fact that most of it was downhill!

Weakness and intestinal upset, tentatively diagnosed by Jesse as "Giardia," a protozoan bacteria, overtake me today, and I feel useless. He says there is some medicine in the first-aid pack to treat it, but it is quite strong and hard on the body. I decide to wait and see if the symptoms persist.

I express that I am uncomfortable about my mounting dependency on him for assistance. He says, "don't worry about it." I do.

The group rests at a serene garden spot by the river's edge just outside of Gandrung. Our short rest stop stretches into a long wait. Our porters are not ahead of us, and they have not yet appeared. Karma Sherpa finally shows up and says that some of the porters have gone on strike for more money. Jesse explains that it is a typical scenario in the mountains. He walks back a ways with Karma to help him do some negotiation, and returns to wait with us again.

The striking porters never show up. Neither does some of our equipment. We do have tents for our camp, but no duffel bags. My tent is jokingly left unpitched by the remaining Sherpas, cornering me into sharing with Jesse for the night. I don't complain.

Day 22

The skies are hazy and the mountain views disappear behind us as we reach the village of Gandrug. Our missing equipment has been recovered, several new porters have joined us, and the crew seems to be complete and harmonious again.

It must have taken hundreds of years to create the intricately terraced hillsides in this area, and they seem to produce abundantly. Most of the people here are busy harvesting and threshing. One lady smooths a fresh mixture of cow dung, mud and water on her "front porch," sort of like a new coat of paint. Nasturtiums and geraniums decorate windows and patios, and there is even a basketball court!

Civilization strikes again.

Day 23

Jesse and I have morning tea together and are entertained by the songs of Himalayan Cuckoos and Laughing Thrushes. In the afternoon I reach a low point after feeling like my insides are coming out, and finally accept a dose of Flagyl from the medical kit. I hope it works fast.

After an enjoyable evening of sing-a-long led by William and his ukulele, I return to my own tent to be alone once again. I contemplate Jesse's boyish face, his generosity, his depth of caring. I remember the years I felt that I could never attract really interesting people, mostly because I thought I was pretty boring myself. I don't feel that way any more, and I'm not even surprised that people actually want to hear what I have to say. I've come of age, somehow, and I wonder what happens now. I'm tempted to just burn my plane ticket, and stay here for a while . . .

Day 24

In the morning we pass several round dwellings with thatched roofs which look like "hobbit" houses, and we play hide-and-seek in tall fields of corn waving in the wind.

When we reach the town of Hyangya there is a sudden wrenching in my soul as the peddlers, and reality, hit. The first view of power poles depresses me, and when the noise and exhaust fumes from vehicles invade my senses, I want nothing more than to turn around.

If the culture shock is this bad for me here, I'll be in real trouble when I get to the U.S.

But none of it can take away all that I have gained here. My eyes have been opened, my body has become strong, and my being has grown in ways which I could not have imagined. I feel more authentically myself than I have ever in my life.

*Not to have known either the mountain or
the desert is not to have known one's self.
Not to have known oneself
is to have known no one.*

Joseph Wood Krutch

"Happy May Day, Fair Maiden"

The mountains line up in hazy splendor for viewing from the New Crystal Hotel in Pokhara. Lamjung Himal, Annapurna IV, Annapurna I, Machupuchare, Annapurna II, South Peak. They look as wistful as I feel at our farewell.

In the hotel garden, the group shares a ceremonious thank you and good-bye with the core group of Sherpas, porters and cooks. We present them with gifts of chocolate and articles of clothing in appreciation for their diligence and their care. In the mountains, they were in charge. Familiar with the territory, at home in the environment. The tables are turned now, and they sit across the circle from us in wrought iron chairs, obviously uncomfortable and out of their element, not to mention having shoes on their feet for the occasion.

Our Sherpa guide Narayan bounces, Bhakta Raj smiles, Karma grunts, Prem grimaces, Tej Badur shrinks, cook Narayan preens. All gestures with which I had become so comfortable on the trek. There, we had all been in it together. Here, we are worlds apart.

That evening I discover that Jesse and I are worlds apart, too. After pacing the floor for a while, saying he has something to tell me, he finally blurts out, "I love you and I hope you can forgive me."

"Forgive you? For what?"

"I never meant to deceive you. Our relationship feels so right. Last year my Nepali girlfriend got pregnant. Her brother begged me to marry her, so that she would not be dishonored in the community. I didn't love her, wasn't even sure the child was mine, but I felt it was the right thing to do. Now you have come into my life . . . " His voice trails off.

I stare at him. I am not sure whether I feel heartbroken or relieved.

May 1st

"Happy May Day, Fair Maiden!" William says, greeting me in a sing-song voice.

We sit on the rooftop of the Yellow Pagoda Hotel in Kathmandu in regal splendor, but there is a missing person among us. Jesse is home with his Nepali family and I think everyone feels the loss of his presence. I also feel the emptiness and apprehension of approaching solo, self-reliant travel again. I have loved being pampered. Oh Mother India! I'm not at all sure I wish to return to your arms again.

At least I won't be bringing my Giardia with me. The medication seems to have worked.

Unfortunately, the group spirit has really deteriorated, and we should have parted company before now. Dinner is a disaster of personality conflicts, saved only by a trip to the Mellow Pie Shop, which mellows us all out.

The next morning I get a shock as the knock on my hotel room door reveals a clean-shaven Jesse in jeans and motorcycle boots. Rain and hail keep us indoors where we continue our conversation of the day before.

"I don't blame you for being angry with me, for thinking I'm a jerk," he says. "You have brought such joy to my life, and I don't want to let it go."

"I'm not angry with you, Jesse. I love you, too. But this is it. I will absolutely not interfere with the commitments you have made to others in your life. I have personally experienced the misery that is the inevitable result of such actions."

We hold each other quietly until it is time for him to leave, and then I watch through the window as "Kathmandu Jesse" departs on his Triumph motorcycle down the narrow streets of the city, a dichotomous contrast to the trekking naturalist of the Himalayas.

I think about him as the storm rages, trying to sort out many things. All I know is that he responded to the inner workings of my being, and the outward expressions of myself, better than anyone I have known before. He understands what I have to say. I mean, he *really* understands. And when he looks at me, I don't need to hide; I don't have to worry about being creative, or beautiful, or accomplished. I can just be me.

In a way, our brief relationship was a fantasy fulfilled. It was like discovering the perfect harmony to the melody of my heart. But, just as the mystical mountains give way to the dusty plains, the realm of fantasy dissolves in the world of reality.

Still, both the magic of the Himalaya and my time with Jesse have given me a new perspective on what I desire for my future. I want to be authentic all the time.

I try to write to family and friends, to do my best to communicate where I have been, what I have seen, who I am; but how can I tell them about this?

There is only the moment to live for, and I have lived each moment this past month in Nepal more completely than I have ever lived. I'm so full inside – the empty spaces and deep crevasses of my life are gone. The effect of all of this has been profound, and I don't know how I will be able to assimilate it into my life at home, or, more importantly, if I even wish to come home.

How do I hold onto the magic I felt up there in the mountains, when the magic was created by not holding on?

The next day I wander alone through Kathmandu, sick at heart, looking for a Tibetan carpet and other souvenirs to buy. I pack and repack my duffle bag and pace the floor of my small room at the Kathmandu Guest House. And I eat.

Kathmandu is really a food paradise, created in part by the many westerners who opened restaurants here in the sixties to satisfy the food cravings of all the travelers on drugs. At least it offers a change from the consistent trekking menu of *dal baht*.

At K.C.'s Restaurant, run by an Australian woman and her Nepali husband, I breakfast on French toast with honey, and return at lunchtime for a grilled cheese, tomato and onion sandwich topped off by banana cake. Another grilled cheese and a slice of chocolate cake at Aunt Jane's provides a late afternoon snack, and supper finds me at the Old Yak & Yeti dipping heavy brown bread into beet borscht with sour cream and chives.

At the end of the day my poor body doesn't know what to think; it feels as badly as my heart. It is then that I realize I have been trying to nurture myself with the wrong food.

I return to the Kathmandu Guest House and its beautiful garden filled with the fragrance of night-blooming jasmine and the colors of pansies, tulips and foxglove.

Sitting down in a quiet corner I meditate for a long time, and am ultimately nourished by the inner food of self-knowledge: I am here today, and I will be gone tomorrow. No point in trying to hold on. It will only bring suffering. Everything is temporary. Moment to moment, the only thing that stays the same is change. Impermanence. *Anicca.*

On the surface it seems a fatalistic philosophy. But the deeper my understanding grows of that truth, the more I realize that it is the only path to true happiness, to liberation.

I am ready to leave Nepal now. Ready to be on my own again.

I send a telegram to Kuldeep in India, whose home I visited many weeks ago in New Delhi, saying that I would like to take him up on his offer to stay for a few days. Jesse gives me a ride me to the airport.

Royal Nepal Airlines to New Delhi. A final wave through the airplane window.

Namaste' Jesse. See you later, Kathmandu. I'll be back to the Himal, Nepal. I still feel your call . . .

*There is this about love: that its memory
is not enough: for the soul retracts if it
does not go on loving; whereas to have
traveled once, however long ago —
provided it was real and not bogus travel -
is enough.*

Freya Stark

Back in Your Arms, Mother India

I arrive at 9:00 p.m. in the steamy Delhi airport. A fast-moving current of passengers propels me toward the exit to find a taxi. When I step outside I am surrounded by a mob of men surging toward me, shouting "This way, Memsahib!" "I will take you, Madam!"

I stand, frozen, not knowing what to do, when over the din I hear my name. Looking around incredulously, I hear it again. A man in a clean white shirt and brown trousers comes forward and introduces himself. It is Kuldeep's driver, there at the airport to pick me up. I almost crumble with relief.

The sea of taxi *wallas* parts and I am escorted to a sleek (for India) black car. As my bag is being stowed away, I sink into the cushions of the back seat with a deep sigh of gratitude and a blessing for my thoughtful host.

How glad I am that I decided to take up his invitation to be his guest when I returned to Delhi. I didn't know just how physically and emotionally drained I would be upon my return from Nepal; how much I would appreciate the comforts of a real home.

Kuldeep welcomes me warmly, tells me he has had a letter from our mutual friend in America, shows me to a cozy room and has his cook spread out a delicious snack.

The treatment is royal and I could not ask for more, except about thirty degrees off the thermometer, which reads 95 degrees Fahrenheit at 10:00 p.m. I fall asleep thinking of the pleasant springtime climate I have left behind in Nepal, the beauty and tranquility of her mountains, the bitter-sweet experience of love.

In the morning India surprises me with an unusual lack of bureaucracy. I go downtown to the bank and, without a hitch, buy more traveler's checks on my Visa card. Then I stop at the office of Korean Airlines, and they agree to extend the validity of my four-month plane ticket for an additional month. The time has gone quickly, and there are a few more places I really want to visit before leaving India.

I am also able to get a call through to my parents, which was totally impossible to do from Kathmandu. It is strange talking to them over such distance and time, and the voice delays make it difficult to understand what is being said. But it is clear that Mom and Dad do not sound happy about my decision to stay longer. I know they won't tell me if something is wrong, but I guess that is their decision to make. I must make my own, and India is where I want to be.

Kuldeep decides that we are going to visit the village of Pushkar in Rajasthan, a few hours drive away. He insists that it is a place I must see, with its sacred lake formed by the tears of Lord Shiva after the death of his wife, Sati. Although I balk because I have other places I want to get to, Kuldeep says that

I will find it very colorful and exciting; and since he is being such a kind host, I consent to the trip.

During the hair-rising automobile ride to get there, I agree: I cannot imagine anything more exciting – or terrifying!

If the rusted auto graveyard along the road is any indication, we are lucky to arrive in one piece. Fortunately, I do find myself fascinated by the natural environment, the brightly painted temples, the proud desert people and their comical camels. Most of all, I am drawn, in my usual way, to the life going on in the streets.

The bazaar in Pushkar is crowded and dusty. Bells jingle loudly as turbaned men with bronze skin and dark handlebar mustaches lead their camels through the narrow lanes. Groups of young women in gaily-colored saris, bejeweled from their noses to their toes, gather in tight knots to gossip and giggle. Bright fabrics, pungent spices, and a vibrant array of other merchandise tumbles from the shelves of tiny makeshift stalls.

I poke through the jumble of goods for sale or trade, but I seek nothing in particular. Stopping to drink a glass of freshly squeezed sugar cane juice, I swirl the raw sweetness on my tongue and just experience the color, movement, sound, and smell swirling around me. Then I see them.

The Pushkar Shoes – Love at First Sight

I am drawn to a corner where a street vendor has spread his wares out on the ground. He is selling shoes. But they are not just ordinary shoes. They are extraordinary shoes. The pungent brown leather is hand stitched, the tops intricately embroidered with blue and pink thread, the toes curved

303

gracefully upward. Made to adorn the foot of a desert nomad, or a perhaps a genie. Magical. Fantastical.

I must have a pair. I point to my favorites. Visions of Arabian Nights float through my head as the shoes make their way into my hands. Oh yes, they are so wonderful, so exotic!

Oh no, they are so big, and so heavy.

I groan inwardly. *I simply cannot carry you with me throughout the rest of this journey.*

But the shoes do not listen. They must have me, too.

I soon walk away with my treasure, two extra pounds of weight in my bag and a question in my mind that has come up over and over on this journey.

What on earth was I thinking?

Two days later I am at the Old Delhi Train Station, bound for Rishikesh at the headwaters of the sacred Ganges. There I will visit a yoga institute, which was one of the original reasons for this journey. I abandon the second class waiting room, with its hordes of holy men and families dining on the floor, in favor of the sparsely populated restaurant on the first class side. I'll have enough of their company all night on the train.

The heat is wilting me. My intestines are rumbling. My menstrual period has been missing for the last four months. But I am looking forward to being at the yoga center and excited about the possibility of coming back in the future for a three-month-long teacher training course.

Anicca. Pendulum swinging. *Anicca.* Impermanence. Equanimity is a subtle thing, the inner balance tenuous.

Again I learn, the greater the expectations, the greater the disappointments.

I created an illusion for myself of what I wanted to find, without any clear understanding of the reality as it exists. It turns out that what I have learned of yoga in the west is only a tendril of what is being taught here. And the plant from which that tendril creeps is not very attractive to me; nor are the people here.

At this *ashram*, yoga practice is intertwined with Hindu religion and ritual. I probably could handle that, taking what I want and leaving the rest, but it's hard for me to get past the extreme Guru worship; and there is a sort of tunnel vision on the part of the disciples that makes it difficult to interact with anyone.

Their eyes are glazed rather than clear, and they seem to move as a unit to the beat of the teacher's drum. The cultish vibration makes my skin crawl. I feel apprehensive, as though there are strange forces around, and that if I do not remain very aware I could become trapped here. It is an eerie sensation.

I realize that I have experienced this discomfort, this inner agitation, in some Hindu temples before, and even on the streets of India at times. But for me, this ashram is the epitome of where I do not want to be. I feel farther away from "home" here than I have felt during my entire journey. I just want to click my heels together and be back in Kansas, or even Kathmandu, again.

Give me Buddha and his peaceful smile any time.

If nothing else, this place has helped to clarify my own path. Being a Jewish Buddhist (who does yoga) feels absolutely right.

After spending a hot, humid night on my wooden plank bed, I walk down to the river near the yoga center and consider taking a dip. The water looks pretty clean, there are no floating animals, and the *ghats* leading to the river are not crowded as in Benares, but who knows what invisible microbes lurk within this part of the Ganges? Throwing caution to the wind, I lower myself into the water. It washes away my stickiness, and, if I choose to believe it, maybe even my sins.

Later, I go into Rishikesh for a watermelon to satisfy my craving, and to look for a pharmacy. My feet have suddenly developed something like athlete's foot all over the soles. They are drying up and peeling.

I find the chemist's shop between the stalls of the barber and the tailor, and I buy a tube of cream after a lengthy exchange with the clerk, whose grave advice is, "Stay out of the river, Madam."

So much for holy water.

In the evening the heat and humidity that have been hanging heavy in the air all day suddenly break as an incredible storm hits. Lightning flashes and thunder crashes, wind bangs at the windows and torrential rain beats down on the roof. Soon the violent sounds outside are accompanied by voices droning the chant *Om Namo Narayanaya* in a room near my own.

Late in the night, as the storm rages on, I am awakened by a tempest in my own body. Doubled over with stomach cramps and dripping with a cold sweat, I run down the hall to the toilet – but I am too late. Horrified and humiliated, I clean myself up and crawl back to bed.

Oh, Mother India, your embrace begins to strangle me . . . .

I rest all the next day. As I lie in bed, I observe the sensations on my body and am aware of the play of *anicca* throughout my being. It is as if I can see myself changing continually, as if I can watch myself aging moment by moment. So temporary, so impermanent.

Then I wonder what it's really like to grow old, and to die; and in the same moment, I know the answer.

Well, it's like . . . this.

For that is exactly what is happening right now. From the moment we're born the same process, always the same process. No amount of attachment, no amount of craving or hoping or praying will alter it. And that's the Truth. I can resist it and be miserable, or I can accept it and be free. The Art of Living, and the Art of Dying.

Anicca. Anicca. Anicca.

The edges of Asia scrape incessantly
against what's common and true to
us in America . . . I'm dying to get out
of here, and I cannot bear the thought
of leaving.

Jeff Goldblum

One Step Back

I regain my strength in a couple of days, and decide to travel to Srinigar in the northernmost part of India. My motivation is not only to see the legendary beauty of the Kashmir Valley, but to use it as a stepping stone to Ladakh, an area known as "Little Tibet," which is high on my list of places to be in India.

The air in Srinigar is pleasantly cool, and the city is a crowded, colorful mixture of Asian cultures. The streets are peppered with ladies completely veiled in black *burkas*, gentlemen in Russian-style wool hats, signs in Persian script, shopkeepers badgering each other and their customers in various languages, and large water-pipes known as *hookahs* being shared by groups of swarthy, bearded men. The small Tibetan refugee center in town includes a factory where laughing, singing women in Tibetan costume weave thick carpets on huge looms while others card, spin and knit sheep and yak wool into bulky sweaters and scarves.

The city sits at the edge of Dal Lake, a large, clear body of water in which the snowy peaks of the Himalayas are reflected.

Rows and rows of houseboats float along the twisting shoreline, making it hard to tell in places exactly where the city ends and the lake begins. Long, narrow boats called *shikaras* glide smoothly over the glassy surface. Some of the boats are filled with merchandise for sale, like floating stores. Others offer cushioned beds on which to recline during a gentle ride across the water to the ancient Mogul gardens.

It is easy to understand why the rulers of the Mogul empire came to the cool, green Kashmir Valley to find relief from the hot plains of India, even four hundred years ago. Their art, architecture, and the stunning formal gardens they created, along with the natural beauty of the valley, make the Vale of Kashmir a place of mystique and romance. Yet it is a place that doesn't hold me.

It is to the higher valleys I want to go, to the Buddhist monasteries and Tibetan culture that call to me, draw me deeply, beyond reason.

So I board a plane the next day to Leh, Ladakh, but bad weather at the other end prevents us from landing. We are forced to return to Srinigar. At the expense of Indian Airlines, until another flight can be scheduled, I have been given accommodation on a lovely houseboat on Dal Lake. The boat is named "Mother India." She definitely helps to ease the disappointment.

An arbor of roses creates an aromatic canopy as I sit on the porch, watching *shikaras* glide by. In the water nearby, perfectly formed lotus blossoms float among a tangle of lily pads. The mountains which embrace the Kashmir Valley are obscured by the dark clouds which keep me from reaching Ladakh.

I am served a Mogul-style lunch of Kashmiri *nan*, a flat bread topped with nuts and raisins, Irani *nan* stuffed with cheese and topped with cream and fruit, and *gushtaba*, lamb meatballs in a buttery yogurt sauce into which to dip the breads. It is the most marvelous food I have had in all of India.

The next day another flight to Leh is attempted, and the mountain views above the thick clouds are magnificent as we fly quite near the snowy peaks. Unfortunately, the landing in Leh is again aborted and we return to Srinigar.

At the airport, a fellow passenger reveals that he heard the pilot was quite lost in the clouds and we were but 200 feet from the mountain walls. No wonder they looked so close! I begin to have mixed feelings about whether it is the right time for me to go to Ladakh.

Frustration is the only reward of trying to get answers from the airlines about when the flight might be attempted next. I decide to take a *shikara* ride across the lake, during which I fall asleep, and later wander through the Moghul splendor of the Shalimar Gardens. Then I go downtown and appease myself with the purchase of intricately painted Kashmiri *papier-maché* boxes at the shop of Suffering Moses.

Upon receipt of the news that another flight to Leh will not be attempted until two days from now, and not for sure at that, I get a strong feeling that my timing isn't right. I decide, sadly, to forego "Little Tibet."

That prompts the refund of my plane ticket, and a trip out of the valley by bus.

Yet, once on the bus, I really can't figure out why I was in such a hurry to leave Kashmir. It becomes clear to me that if I truly understood the truth of *anicca* I would simply observe the impermanence and changing of every phenomenon in every moment, and I wouldn't have to make so many moves myself.

It also seems since my return to India that I have become more narrow minded instead of more open minded. I notice that I have less patience and less interest in where I am. I am aware that I am prejudiced, and I know what I like. I can barely meditate for the agitation and constant thoughts. I'm rushing around again, when I don't need to. I don't know where I want to be. In some ways I'm looking forward to America, and I don't want to be there at all. Wanting desperately to visit more places, not caring whether I do or not.

I thought I had come so far, gotten myself "together." Now I feel about as enlightened as a mirror shattered into a zillion fragments. So goes *anicca*.

It is clear that the mental process of change is no different than the physical process I observed the other night. No state of mind remains the same for long. One moment tranquil, the next overwhelmed. Happy. Sad. Angry. Ecstatic. Depressed.

And even as I feel disappointed in myself for not maintaining a balanced mind, the awareness that equanimity has eluded me once again brings my inner lens back into focus. Makes the picture clearer. For a moment. Focus. Refocus. A constant process. I feel like I've taken one step back; but now I know that this, too, shall pass.

Two steps forward coming up.

The bus ride to Jammu takes about ten hours on a bright clear day — a precarious ride down an inordinately busy and precipitous road. I shrink down into my seat, only occasionally daring to peek through the grimy windows to see reflections of snow-capped mountains in flooded rice paddies being plowed by water buffalo. The Vale of Kashmir appears to be almost completely immersed in water.

The bus teeters on the steep edge of the sharply curving roadway as we climb out of the huge valley. I am thrown forward, backward and sideways in my seat by innumerable lurching stops and starts, careening turns, games of chicken.

My gasps of fright at the thought of being splattered all over the road are interspersed with occasional cheers from the crowd of passengers when the driver gets us through a tight situation successfully.

Both terrifying and ridiculous, the bus rides of India are some of my very favorite experiences in this country: the glimpses of village life, the roadside tea stalls, the ragged turbans and jeweled noses, the questioning looks, the welcoming smiles.

Risky – but worth it. Then again, what isn't?

. . . peculiar travel suggestions
are dancing lessons from God.

Kurt Vonnegut

No Excuses

I disembark in Jammu and face a crossroads of choices. A side trip to the Golden Temple of the Sikhs at Amritsar? Or straight on to the village of Dharamsala – home in exile of the Dalai Lama, the religious leader of Tibet. After setting up a train reservation to Amritsar, I instinctively do a quick turn-about and hop a train in the direction of Dharamsala instead. Perhaps I have finally learned something. The Buddhist destination wins out.

Arriving late at Pathankot station, I spend the night on a bench in the railway waiting room in order to catch the 5:00 a.m. coach to Dharamsala. Sore and sleepless, it seems as if morning will never come.

Yet, once aboard the bus, I am wide awake with anticipation, for I have heard wonderful things about the Tibetan refugee community nestled into the foothills of the Indian Himalayas. I need to sit down and relax, to stay in one place for a while. There is nowhere else I wish to go now, nothing more important than just to be.

A whole new group of passengers piles on the bus when we reach the "lower" part of split-level Dharamsala, and I am surrounded by smiling faces full of pride and curiosity, with the high cheekbones, strong jaws, almond eyes and uniquely shaped heads of the Tibetan people. I feel a tremendous surge of happiness as the bus continues up the sharp grade to "upper" Dharamsala, the Tibetan community known as MacLeod Ganj.

What a relief it is to be in Buddha-land again!

I walk by the huge prayer wheel in the center of town, inhale the smell of freshly baked brown bread, see the rows of prayer flags flipping around in the wind, and gaze up at the snow-tipped mountains rising above. It is a lot like being in a Nepali village. I look forward to becoming familiar with the people, the shops, the restaurants, the Tibetan Library and Archives and the hiking trails into the foothills. Perhaps I will even have a *baku*, a Tibetan dress, stitched up for myself.

Lia, a German woman to whom I was referred by my friend Arlene in America, agrees to rent me a room for two weeks in a small compound she owns above McLeod.

She directs me up a steep path which winds into the trees above the town. After about a mile, I recognize the low stone wall which she described as a landmark to identify her property. Carrying my duffle up the steep hill takes my last ounce of energy, and leaves me dying for a bath. However, I soon discover that there is no running water on the property. The English woman staying in the next cottage hands me a plastic bucket and describes the way to the well, a quarter-mile straight down the hill behind the compound. I decide to temporarily forgo the bath in favor of a rest.

What I need to do here is spend some quiet time putting myself back together. I've been looking too much ahead again, worrying about what the future holds and having real trouble staying in the present moment. The timeless feeling of Nepal has dissipated, and the effortless floating begins to feel like a struggle to keep my head above the surface again. One thing feels good: the PAST no longer haunts me. But I know that obsessive thoughts about what comes next are not healthy either, and perhaps the time here will provide an antidote.

Meditation practice is also an objective. Now I have the time, the place, and no excuses.

After a short rest, I make my trip down to the well and back up again, arms aching from the weight of the water bucket up the steep incline. But now, hair washed, body washed, clothes washed, I'm a new woman! My room is sunny and my only real problem is the mosquitoes, which are quickly eating me alive. I'm discovering that believing in *karma*, even as it pertains to killing mosquitoes, can make life difficult. In the long run, though, I know my understanding of "what goes around comes around," or, as Goenka explained it, "as the seed is, so the fruit shall be," will make life much easier.

My room is named "Sunset." A skylight welcomes the sun to warm and light the space, and creates a musical score of pattering raindrops in the afternoon.

At 4:00 a dark-haired young western woman appears at my door with a pot of tea. Twenty-three-year-old Elizabeth from Spain lives in another one of the small cottages that dot the property around the main house. She is a student of Tibetan Buddhism and *Vipassana* meditation and has been in

Dharamsala for several months.

She tells me that many Westerners spend time in MacLeod Ganj studying at the Tibetan Library founded by the Dalai Lama, because this is about as close to the source of Tibetan Buddhism as they can possibly come.

Noticing that I have not yet purchased food supplies, she tells me to "wait a minute," and returns shortly with a delightful meal of fresh *chapatis* and vegetables, including tofu, potatoes, okra, tomatoes and onions, all topped with cheese and hot off the kerosene burner. It is just perfect! Both the food, and the companionship.

I sleep deeply and peacefully, and in the morning Elizabeth appears again. She offers me a place on her thickly woven Tibetan carpet, spread out in the sun beneath the pines and within the sound of the Himalayan cuckoo, while she prepares tea and bread with butter and honey for my breakfast. For some reason, she feels that I need this kind of care right now. She is right. I think she needs someone to care for, too.

Back in my little abode after a shopping trip to town, it is clear that I purchased more fresh fruit and vegetables than I can possibly eat before they spoil. Well, I can share some with Elizabeth, and at least I'll be self-sufficient for a few days and not have to go out again soon.

The short journey exhausted me, and it wasn't because of the walk. It was because I met and spoke with several people from Australia, Canada, Europe and America along the way.

I realize that expressing myself thoughtfully and truthfully, as opposed to idle chit-chat, is work. Mental work, and spiritual work. I'm also listening more carefully to what people are saying, and considering my responses, instead of offering stock

322

answers or platitudes. And I don't want to hear any gossip, which seems to be a focus of much conversation among the Westerners.

Maybe it's because I've been alone a lot lately, but silence is definitely easier and more comfortable for me.

Living in the present moment becomes reality. Meditation from 6:30 to 7:30 a.m. A clear mind and happy thoughts when thoughts arise, only to pass away into awareness of the sensations of my body, the impermanence of my being. A short yoga session reminds my body of sun salutations and gentle stretches. Then come the moments of lighting the kerosene stove, preparing coffee, spreading bread with butter and honey, scrambling an egg. I never realized what pure enjoyment there could be in the moment-to-moment awareness of cooking, and eating, an egg. A walk to the toilet room to rid my body of yesterday's wastes. Sitting outdoors in the morning warmth with a good book. Dish washing, teeth brushing, body cleansing and anointing. Living. Being. It's 10:00 a.m. My day already feels full, complete.

Though I am doing "nothing," I'm so aware of every moment that I feel more productive than when I'm doing "something!"

In the afternoon I walk mindfully and meditatively up the hill from the well holding a full bucket of water balanced precariously on one shoulder. I'm not yet ready to balance it on my head, but I've found it too hard on my arms to carry it the "western" way. As I reach the top of the hill, I gloat with satisfaction at having made it without spilling more than a few drops. A moment later, I get my just reward for that display of pride and ego. The bucket falls out of my hands, and all but a trickle of that lovingly carried water ends up on the ground.

With a wry smile, I understand then what is jokingly referred to as "instant karma." Sometimes the "seed" (the mental action, the cause) seems to produce the "fruit" (results, the effect) instantly. In other words, it doesn't always take lifetimes to get what you deserve.

Presents for myself. A Tibetan *jhola* (shoulder bag) and a small gong etched with the symbols of the blessings of the Buddha, which rings with a clear and penetrating tone. A healthy lunch of vegetables and tofu. After a diet of mostly grains and potatoes in Nepal, my body yearns for fresh vegetables and fruit. I'm hoping that good food and being in one place for a while will encourage my monthly period to return once again.

At Elizabeth's suggestion, I stop in at the Tibetan Medical Center, where I tell Dr. Dolma about the cessation of my menstrual cycle as she busily separates herbs and puts them into plastic bags. She comes over to where I sit, her dark braid draped gracefully over her shoulder to her waist, and has me stick out my tongue. Her almond shaped eyes look deeply into my own as she listens to the pulses in both my wrists with her fingers. Then she quickly writes out a prescription in Tibetan script and sends me to the "pharmacy" in the next room. Soon I am on my way again, with a bag of brown pills which look like rabbit pellets. I am told they will purify my blood and help it start flowing again.

As I head back up the hill, the sky turns a menacing yellow-gray. The wind blows wildly and the monkeys in the trees start to scream. Suddenly I am pelted mercilessly by the heaviest raindrops and biggest hailstones I've ever seen. I take cover under the canopy of a tree and watch the thunderous clouds move across the sky. In ten minutes, the storm is over. It is a sign that the monsoon season is approaching.

When the rain stops, I continue on to the nearby house of Lama Ling Rimpoche, an aging monk whom I have been told sees westerners once a week to answer their spiritual questions and give his blessings. He is a venerable, sweet old soul, and is assisted by a devoted young monk as translator.

I come with no particular concerns, but I am happy to receive blessings. He advises me to study hard and practice continuously. Then he gives me a "protection knot" of red string to tie around my neck.

Alhough I have no idea exactly what I'm being protected from, I don't plan to take it off and find out.

The warm sun feels like a healing balm on the many itchy bug bites which plague me, as I sit on my little patio reading and writing.

My Tibetan neighbor Pala is the caretaker of this property. He sits on his porch fingering the prayer beads of his *mala*, sighing deeply and repeatedly chanting *Om! Mani Padme Hum!* He meditates for hours at a time like that, his *mantra* vibrating on the wind and into my own heart. Occasionally he stops for a bit to mend a fence or water some flowers, but he returns immediately to his spot on the porch, picks up his beads and resumes. Is that devotion? Faith? Surrender?

I recall something Elizabeth said to me during one of our discussions about meditation, when I was expressing some doubt and wondering why I keep on meditating even when my knees are searing with pain and my mind is cajoling me to stop.

"Until you begin to realize some benefit from the practice, it doesn't always make sense."

That makes perfect sense.

I want to write to some good friends, but I don't know what to say. Everything I think and feel seems to involve my experiences here. How will I be able to relate to those at home?

All that we see or seem
Is a dream within a dream.

Edgar Allan Poe

An Inner Door Left Ajar

Today is May 29. It is also the fifteenth day of the fourth month on the Tibetan Calendar: the day on which Buddha's birth, enlightenment, and passage into *nirvana* all coincide. People stream down to the Tibetan Library for the celebration. It's definitely not your typical birthday party.

The *puja* consists of several hours of chanting and offerings. The lama intones verses of Tibetan scripture and then waits while the mostly-Western crowd chants a response. He holds the ritual objects of Bell in one hand and *Dorji* in the other. Elizabeth explains that the Bell represents the creative force in the universe, or the female energy, and the *Dorji,* which is shaped to represent the force of a two-sided bolt of lightning, signifies the masculine energy. Together, they can restore harmony within the universe.

While chanting, the lama moves the sacred objects into various positions. These *mudras*, or hand movements, are like an intricate, sacred choreography.

As the formal rituals come to an end, the lama's sparkling eyes scan the crowd of devotees. He seems to be filled to the top with glee, and I think he is silently roaring with laughter inside. My impression is that he gets a kick out of the sincerely serious, extremely devoted, but in-too-much-of-a-hurry-to-get-enlightened Westerners.

The morning dawns clear after an intense rainstorm during the night. Lightning flashed through the skylight creating surreal patterns in the room and in my mind, the whole scene keeping me awake for some time.

During the day, my meditation experiences vary. Some hours are filled with chattering thoughts, continually arising to distract my attention. Sometimes the pain in my legs from sitting cross-legged is incredibly intense; yet I sit perfectly still, observing the sensations and striving for equanimity, even when I want to scream.

Sometimes I find a very calm place, as I move my awareness within and throughout my body and mind. And one time an inner doorway comes into view, opening to a place I haven't entered before. A very soft, vulnerable place. A place which seems to speak to me.

> *You've reached the threshold*
> *the door's ajar*
> *Please, open gently*
> *and not too far*
> *There's fear attached to opening wide*
> *It's just too tender there*
> *inside.*

Continuing carefully, I move my awareness deeper and deeper to my inner core through layers of my being, reaching levels of knowing that are far beyond what I can synthesize with my consciousness, and experience my nature as pure essence, as ethereal beingness unfettered by body and mind. Limitless. Eternal.

Until my awareness is suddenly ambushed.

Wait a minute! Where am I? Who am I? Is anybody home in there?

In a moment, the experience of self-realization dissolves into memory, the inner door closing gently – but not quite all the way. My ego seems to sigh with relief, and my mind shares the root of its fear:

> *Knowing not what is my fate,*
> *I fear "I" might*
> *dis in te grate.*

And what remains when "I" am gone? Who will I be if not the me I've known and loved (occasionally) for so long?

All the artfully created labels of my life, my carefully constructed persona – these have no effect whatsoever upon the ultimate truth, the reality which simply is.

But what does this mean for my life?

For one thing, it means that I'm in on the joke. That I can sport the labels and wear the image, as long as I don't take it seriously and become attached to the ideas of "me" and "mine." For they are truly illusions. The source of misery. The seeds of *karma*.

It means that, although I live in the world of apparent reality, I must maintain awareness of the ultimate reality, and know that I have a choice in every moment to remain aware and balanced, and live my life in a positive way that will be uplifting to myself and to all those around me.

It means that whatever it was I experienced in there has moved me from the arena of doubt into the realm of faith.

That night I have a dream. A lucid dream. A dream of death, and rebirth.

Three women climb a tall, narrow ladder to the top of a very high tower. I am the one in the middle. We are there to jump to our deaths – to join loved ones who have been killed in a fire. Below us is a wooden platform, much like a stage. We prepare as if to take off on a high dive, with a-one, and a-two, and a-three, running forward to leap off the tower.

Arms out to the sides in freefall style, the two women on either side of me descend at a faster rate than I. Suddenly I see them hit the stage. They splatter onto the wooden surface, becoming big spreading purple blotches of protoplasm.

Realizing that I will also shortly hit, and not wanting to land on top of one of them, I try to focus on landing square in the empty space between them. The stage looms closer as I gain speed.

At that moment I have the awareness that I am dreaming, and think to myself "you always wake up before something like this happens because you don't know what it's like to die."

I am in for a surprise.

I feel the impact of the hard surface, and then I, too, "splatter." There are sensations of oozing, fluidity and warmth as "I" begin to flow out of my body. There is no pain; on the contrary the sensations are quite pleasant. I am enveloped in

332

warm, thick, viscous fluid. More accurately, I am this oozing, flowing substance.

My body is destroyed, but my consciousness is in heightened awareness. I am in awe, and I think in the dream how amazing it is that I am still "conscious" and aware of these sensations when I am obviously dead, and how incredible it is that I feel no pain. Most astounding is the freedom of the formlessness which I have become.

After a short while, I see the women on either side of me re-form into their physical shapes, like a movie running backwards. They get up, and walk away. I then do the same thing. I gather the majority of myself together, and, leaving bits and pieces of myself which I no longer need behind me on the stage, I walk away.

I wake up knowing what it means. Time to let go. Time to die to old ways of being, outdated mind sets, useless paradigms. Time for transformation. Time for rebirth.

The days begin to drag as I get caught in the space between here and there. Knowing it's getting close, not wanting to think about it: going back to America. I try not to buy too much food, feel too settled, create any new habits.

And I wonder how I will answer the inevitable question, "How was your trip?" in ten words or less . . .

The farther she traveled into unknown places, unfamiliar places, the more precisely she could find within herself a map showing only the cities of the interior.

Anais Nin

Taking Refuge

The morning of my departure from MacLeod Ganj I am taken by Nina, an American woman who lives in another of the cottages near mine, to see her guru. He is a Tibetan Buddhist lama named Chamdo Geshe. Nina explains that *Geshe* means teacher, and she refers to him affectionately as *Geshe-la*.

I have seen little of Nina since my arrival, and we have spoken only a few times. She spends most of her hours in meditation and devotional practice, and studying Tibetan language to better understand the scriptures and converse with her teacher. She is very devoted to him and believes he is a truly enlightened being. It is her gift to me, as I prepare to leave the compound, the village and the country itself, to introduce me to *Geshe-la* and receive the benefit of his blessing.

It is a cool, clear day, and the monk's simple hut of mud bricks and thatched roof is a short walk down the road from our cottages. As we cross the threshold, my eyes take a moment to adjust from the brightness outside. The dim room has no electricity, but I soon see that it needs none, for an aura of light emanates from the man himself. I have never seen such clarity in a pair of eyes, such compassion in a smile.

337

Nina has told me that he is around fifty, but his face appears ageless, expressing both the innocence of a child and the wisdom of a sage. I bathe in his welcoming gaze, momentarily mesmerized, until Nina gently nudges me, breaking the lovely spell.

I am reminded to hold out my gift of a *kata,* a scarf of white gauzy cloth, which I am told is the appropriate offering to bring to a lama. Eyes sparkling, he places both of his hands together near his heart and bows his shaven head so that I may place the strip of cotton around his neck. Then, his dark orange robes rustling around him, he prepares Tibetan butter tea for our refreshment. It is a slightly rancid concoction, and I try not to grimace as it slides down my throat and leaves an oily coating in my mouth.

I notice a small statue of a Tibetan goddess sitting on a high shelf. Nina explains that she is *Tara,* the Goddess of Protection.

"When *Geshe-la* fled Tibet after the invasion of the Chinese in 1951, all he was able to take with him was that statue, which he hid within the folds of his robes. He is sure that is why he escaped with his life."

Chamdo Geshe proceeds to address me in Tibetan. He looks at me closely, and his eyes seem to be simultaneously searching and knowing, serious and laughing, if that is possible. Nina translates his question for me, and my reply for him.

"Why have you come here?" he asks.

"To receive your blessing for my journey home."

Nodding slowly, he then has Nina tell me that he will perform a ritual to invoke the protection of the Goddess *Tara* to see me safely on my journey.

338

His eyes close halfway as he begins to chant, and his hands flow gracefully into a series of *mudras*, the sacred positions. I feel my heart open to receive the blessing; it is as if his chant, his light, his depth of compassion act as a gentle solvent to the psychic crustiness beginning to form again.

When he is finished, he teaches me the *mantra* so that I am able to invoke *Tara's* protection whenever I need it. *Om Tar-ray Tu-tar-ray Tu-ray So-ha.*

Then he takes my hand and tells me to say the *Tara mantra* whenever I am traveling. He kisses my hand in farewell and looks intently into my eyes. Nina translates his next words with a puzzled look.

"Be sure to always say the *mantra* when you are on a bus." His eyes are not laughing now, and a drop of concern ripples through my calmness. Still, as I leave him, I feel wonderful, and truly blessed.

Taking his advice to heart, I chant the *mantra* from the moment I board the bus in McLeod all the way down the winding hillside road through Dharamsala to Pathankot. I continue to chant on the train to Delhi, and even in the scooter *ricksha* I take from place to place around the city on my last day in India.

I know it's important to remember to use the *mantra*. The look on *Geshe-La's* face told me so.

The Pushkar Shoes – We Meet Again

It is 9:00 p.m. and 90 degrees in New Delhi. I am due at the airport in less than an hour for my flight back to America, and I'm still not packed.

Struggling to jam everything into my bag, I berate myself for having accumulated so much during my five months in India and Nepal. Frustrated, I pull everything out and dump it all on the floor. At the top of the pile is the pair of hand-made embroidered leather shoes I bought at the Pushkar bazaar on a whim.

Seeing those crazy shoes suddenly makes me angry. Just another one of my compulsive, useless purchases. Like the bells, the saris, the woodcarvings. What will I ever do with them anyway? I have stacks of items from previous travels stored away already. Souvenirs I had thought I simply could not live without; material things to somehow substantiate the value of my journeys, my life, my Self. As if *I* were not enough.

The shoes are so heavy, and smell like camel dung and smoke and spices. Smells which nauseate me in my anxiety about returning home after all this time to an unknown future. I resentfully wrap them in an Indian cotton scarf and stuff them deep into my bag.

Still, as I prepare to fly away from India, the things I contemplate amaze me. I think about renunciation of "worldly" life, not in a cave or a monastery, but in a definite commitment to the *Dhamma*, the Truth, the Art of Living. I think about joining a *sangha*, a community which will support and share my commitment. But how to begin? That is the question.

You have begun. That is the answer.

I board Alitalia Airlines to Bangkok. What a treat.

Namaste' chapatis and *chai.*

Bon giorno croissants and *cappuccino!*

Um, what was I saying about renunciation?

During my one-day stopover in Bangkok, I get to experience what so many others have told stories about. I thought I was immune. Don't we all?

I no longer have my ticket, my passport, or my traveler's checks. Foolishly, the last day of the journey, I pack away my money belt. Throwing everything into my Tibetan shoulder bag, I climb aboard a congested city bus. Passengers push and shove and press around me tightly. When the crowd thins, I discover that my bag has been slit open and everything removed. So carefully, that I felt nothing.

It was the first time I had forgotten to say the *Tara mantra* on a bus.

I see the face of *Geshe-La* floating before my eyes, looking at me intently with concern. How did he know? Could he really have foreseen?

My skin crawls with the sensations of agitation.

I make a report at the Lumphini Police Station: agitation. I apply for a new passport at the American Embassy: agitation. A new visa at Thai immigration: agitation. A new ticket at Korean Airlines: agitation. New travelers checks at the Bank of America: agitation. My awareness is scattered, my equanimity is gone, my ability to meditate is nil. My fragmented mind races back and forth, east to west, west to east, lost in the time space between the worlds.

On Korean Air Lines to Los Angeles at last. The clouds below look like fantasy mountains rising from turbulent oceans, thick and fluffy, like great heaps of snow and powdery mist hanging in space.

The past five months flash through my memory and vibrate in my cells as I re-read the pages of my journals and recall the images impressed upon my mind. But I realize that they are only the words and pictures of the journey.

Closing my eyes, I search through my being for an understanding of what I have gained, what I am bringing home with me.

What I find is my breath, coming in, going out; my bodily sensations, arising and passing away; my awareness of change, of impermanence, of being, becoming, being, becoming, *anicca, anicca, anicca.*

I know that I have traveled too far on my inner journey to ever go back; and I don't really want to go back. Yet, I am fearful of going forward. It feels like too strange and foreign a landscape. Much bigger, and riskier, than Asia. Something tells me that I am entering unknown territory; a region for which there is no guidebook. And I don't know if I can go there alone.

Who, and what, will guide me now?

Where will I find refuge from the inevitable storms?

As if in answer, some words float softly through my thoughts. They are the words I was asked to repeat on the first day of the ten-day *Vipassana* meditation course with Goenka, an eternity ago. Words I once resisted, rejected, misunderstood. Words of devotion. Words of protection. Words of surrender.

I chant them silently to myself, as the landing gear grinds into position . . .

342

"I take refuge in *Buddha*."

    The qualities of enlightenment.

"I take refuge in *Dhamma*."

    The law, the universal truth.

"I take refuge in *Sangha*."

    The community of people who walk the path.

. . . and I welcome myself home.

May all of you enjoy real happiness.
May all beings be happy.

S. N. Goenka

From the Heights of the Himalayas

The following letter reached home shortly after I did.

Dear Family,

Asia has fascinated me, inspired me and exhausted me.

It has taken me from the heights of the Himalayas to the depths of the mind, and beyond. Such have been the contrasts of this journey; such have been the contrasts of my life.

In your letters, you have encouraged me to "have fun" and to "relax." Yet the truth is, to be here is not to have fun. To sit in silent meditation is not to relax. Well then, you may ask, what is the purpose of the journey? The answer is elusive, and does not lend itself well to words. Still, words are all I have to attempt to share my experience here with you.

This land, by its very nature, is intensely challenging and stimulating, and the teachings it offers are profound. Why do I choose to be challenged, stimulated and taught in this way? Because it is my wish to explore beyond the known to the unknown; to broaden the boundaries of my universe; to see the world from the top of the mountain instead of always living within its shadow.

347

My meditation teacher has said that when light is present, darkness must go; so also, with the development of wisdom, ignorance must go. In my own ignorance, I have created a lot of misery for myself and for so many others in my life; for I could see only from one angle – the bottom of the mountain.

Now, more than just my desire, it seems my responsibility, my obligation, to develop my own wisdom and come out of ignorance – as much for the benefit of others as myself. My meditation practice is the foundation of this process, and has become an invaluable part of my life.

I deeply appreciate your support as I continue to walk this path of self-knowledge, liberation, and inner peace.

With gratitude, and with love, always.

Namaste'

I honor the place in you in which
the entire universe dwells.
I honor the place in you which is of
love, of light, of truth and of peace.
I honor the place in you where
if you are in that place in you
and I am in that place in me,
then we are one.

Indian Salutation

"Sole" Mates

The morning is clear and bright in quiet suburban Southern California as I open the front door and retrieve the newspaper from the porch. Turning back into the house, I see them next to the welcome mat. A pair of intricately embroidered hand-stitched leather shoes that reached out to me once upon a time in a dusty desert bazaar in India.

The Pushkar Shoes look worn and faded now from exposure to the elements, almost as if they had been worn by the desert nomad for whom they were intended.

Myriad feelings wash over me each time I spy them there on the step, along with memories, visions and impressions of the sights and smells of a land far away. A land whose impact upon my spirit was profound.

I returned to India again after two years for another seven months, but that's a story for another time. I also married once more and we have a daughter. We travel as a family now.

Sometimes it seems as if I have lived several different lives within this very lifetime. Yet here, at the threshold of today, the presence of the Pushkar Shoes serves to remind me of all the steps I have taken, and have yet to take, along this winding path of life.

Afterword

Over the years, I have kept walking on the path of *Vipasssana* meditation. It continues to enhance my life immeasurably.

At the time of this first journey in 1980, the only centers offering courses in *Vipassana* meditation as taught by S. N. Goenka were located in India. At the time of this writing, many years later, there are more than 150 established *Vipassana* meditation centers around the world. Each center follows the same guidelines, and every ten-day course is still essentially taught by S. N. Goenka (preserved through the miracle of digital technology). Each meditation center is also an independently operated non-profit organization established by students of *Vipassana* meditation who have realized benefit from their practice, and wish to make the experience of the *Dhamma* available to as many people as possible. As always, and in every location, there is never a charge to take a course in *Vipassana* meditation as taught by S. N. Goenka. All centers are served by volunteers and operated on a donations-only basis.

For more information about *Vipassana* meditation, or to find a *Vipassana* meditation center located near you, please visit: www.dhamma.org

15188230R00215

Printed in Great Britain
by Amazon